The
Green
Belt
Memory
Jogger®

A Pocket Guide
for Six Sigma DMAIC
Success

First Edition GOAL/QPC

The Green Belt Memory Jogger®

Six Sigma is a federally registered trademark of Motorola, Inc.
Minitab® is a trademark of Minitab, Inc.

Development Team:

Author: Sarah A. Carleton
Project Management: John Hamilton
Design and Layout: Margaret MacLennan
Editor: Francine Oddo
Proofreader: Susan Griebel, Alex Druckmiller

GOAL/QPC
13 Branch Street, Suite 103, Methuen, MA 01844
800.643.4316 or 603.893.1944
service@goalqpc.com

www.goalqpc.com

Printed in the United States of America

First Edition

10 9 8 7 6 5

ISBN: 978-1-57681-176-4

Acknowledgments

Our sincerest thanks to the people and organizations who contributed content, suggestions, review feedback, and encouragement or who gave us permission to adapt their charts, tables, and other information.

We are indebted to the following contributors and reviewers to this and/or earlier editions who ensured that the finished book aligned with expectations: Paul Sheehy, Daniel Navarro, Robert Silvers, Victoria Keyes, Deb Dixon, Six Sigma Academy; Lyn Dolson Pugh, Katherine Calvert, Michael G. Thibeau, Dow Chemical Company; Larry R. Smith, Ford Motor Company; Marc Richardson, JAE Oregon, Inc.; Kristi Brown, WalMart; David M. Oberholtzer, Raytheon Company; Richard K. Bergeron, Seagate Inc.; Raj Gohil, AT&T Corporate Quality; Rip Stauffer, BlueFire Partners; Jeff Karl, Bombardier Regional Aircraft; C. Gregory Brown, Citigroup; Randy Fach, Dove Consulting; Kui-Sun Yim, Ford Motor Company; Cheryl Rienzo, Honeywell, Inc.; David Fogelson, Honeywell, Inc.; Eric Jakubowski, Motorola, Inc.; John Thomasson, NCR Corporation; Russell Soukup, Pemstar, Inc.; Bill Fechter, Ph.D., Productivity Inc.; Jay P. Patel, Quality & Productivity Solutions, Inc.; Allen C. Rothman, Quad Tech, Inc.; Lynda Owens, Neal Mackertich, Raytheon Company; Swaminathan Balachandran, University of Wisconsin–Platteville.

Foreword

GOAL/QPC has a long and valued history of producing essential Memory Joggers® in the fields of Quality, Improvement, Project Management, and skill development.

The Green Belt Memory Jogger® is derived from and aligned with *The Black Belt Memory Jogger*® *Second Edition*. There are several new chapters covering topics, such as Voice of the Customer, Project Benefit Assessment, Risk Assessment, Solution Selection, and Piloting Solutions.

The contents of *The Green Belt Memory Jogger*® are aligned with the ASQ Six Sigma Body of Knowledge and the LSS 6001 - Lean & Six Sigma Black Belt Training International Standard. Each of the tools has been organized into their appropriate phase of the Define, Measure, Analyze, Improve, Control (DMAIC) model to assist in executing projects.

You can rest assured that you have in your hands the right tools, explained in the right way, to make you successful in the field of Six Sigma. With your company Black Belts using *The Black Belt Memory Jogger*® *Second Edition* and the Green Belts using *The Green Belt Memory Jogger*® you can be confident that the mentoring and learning will be of high quality and high consistency as they will all be reading off the same page.

We wish you every success and much learning in your Six Sigma journey.

GOAL/QPC

About the Author

Sarah Carleton is a certified Master Black Belt and the principal of Sarah A. Carleton Consulting, providing lean and six sigma training and mentoring, directly and as a consultant/trainer for GOAL/QPC. She has 35 years of experience as an engineer, manager, and trainer in the lighting and healthcare industries. She has trained over 1000 practitioners, Green Belts, Black Belts, and Master Black Belts in classroom settings and has reached thousands more through e-learning. She has a BA in physics from Middlebury College and an MS in electrical engineering from Northeastern University. She holds 8 patents and has written several publications in the field of lighting. She hopes that this publication helps you increase your knowledge, develop your skills, grow a culture of improvement, and achieve your Green Belt certification.

TABLE OF CONTENTS

TABLE OF CONTENTS

How to Use
The Green Belt
Memory Jogger®

This Memory Jogger® is designed for you to use as a convenient and quick reference guide. The **"Why use it?"**, **"What does it do?"**, and **"How do I do it?"** format offers you an easy way to navigate through the information in each chapter.

Use this guide as a reference on the job, during and after your training, or as part of a self-study program. Put your finger on any individual concept, tool, or section within seconds.

If you are interested in a specific topic, refer to the chapter title pages at the bottom right of each odd numbered page.

Jogger Positions

Getting Ready — When you see the "getting ready" position of the runner, expect a brief description of the tool or task.

Cruising — When you see this runner, expect to find guidelines and interpretation tips. This is the action phase that provides you with step-by-step instructions.

Finishing the Course — When you see this runner, expect to see the tool in its final form with examples to illustrate the application of the tool.

SIX SIGMA AND THE DMAIC MODEL

What is Six Sigma?

Six Sigma refers to a business philosophy, an improvement methodology, and a performance metric. The Six Sigma business philosophy is an initiative that enables world-class quality and continuous improvement to achieve the highest level of customer satisfaction. The Six Sigma methodology utilizes data and statistical tools within a phased approach to improve process performance. The Six Sigma metric establishes a world-class performance level that helps align an organization's strategic goals and values to its customers' needs and expectations.

Sigma (σ) is a measure of the variability of a process with respect to specification limits. In business, a sigma value represents how well a process is performing and how often a defect is likely to occur. The higher the sigma value, the less variation and fewer defects the process will have. Six Sigma is the new standard of excellence at only 3.4 defects per million opportunities (DPMO).

How does it work?

The Six Sigma philosophy uses data and statistical tools to systematically improve processes and sustain process improvements. Process metrics are evaluated based on a comparison of average and variation to performance specifications or targets.

The methodology is a project-focused approach consisting of five phases: Define, Measure, Analyze, Improve, and Control (DMAIC). In the *Define* phase, projects are selected from business, operational, and customer needs, based on their linkage to executive strategies. In the *Measure* phase, tools are applied to validate the measurement system and to characterize the process. In the *Analyze* and *Improve* phases, sources of variation are identified, a statistical relationship between the process input and output variables is established, and the process performance is optimized. The *Control* phase applies traditional and statistical tools to sustain process improvements. Emphasis is placed on controlling the key process inputs to consistently achieve key process outputs.

The DMAIC Model

What is it?

The DMAIC model comprises five phases and specific tools that are used to characterize and optimize both business and industrial processes. Each project must complete the five phases in chronological order.

Define Phase

In the Define phase, the customer needs are defined and the processes and products to be improved are identified.

DEFINE		
Step	**Tools**	**Outputs**
Understand voice of the customer (VOC)	Baseline research, interviews, focus groups, surveys	Prioritized customer needs
Assess business benefits	Project Benefit Assessment	List of project benefits
Define problem	Critical To (CT) Flowdown, IS-IS NOT analysis	Focused problem statement
Define process	SIPOC	Defined process boundaries
Define change management strategy and select team	Change Management, stakeholder management, team building	Change strategy, stakeholder strategy, communication plan, project team
Define project scope and approve charter	Project Charter	Approved project charter

Measure Phase

The Measure phase determines the baseline and target performance of the process, defines the input/output variables of the process, and validates the measurement systems.

MEASURE		
Step	**Tools**	**Outputs**
Map as-is process and look for quick wins	Process Mapping, value stream map	Process map
Prepare data collection plan	Data Collection template	Data collection plan
Analyze measurement system	Gauge calibration, Gauge R&R studies	Validated measurement systems
Analyze process stability and capability	Time series plot, Process Capability studies	Process performance metrics
Manage risk and reconfirm charter	Risk Assessment and Management, Project Charter	Risk management plan, reconfirmed charter

Analyze Phase

The Analyze phase uses data to establish the key process inputs that affect the process outputs.

ANALYZE		
Step	**Tools**	**Outputs**
Identify potential root causes	Process Mapping, Cause & Effect Diagram, Cause & Effect Matrix, IS-IS NOT analysis	List of potential root causes
Stratify and plot process data	Graphical Analysis	Graphs of sources of variation
Confirm root causes with data and statistics	Hypothesis Testing, Regression Analysis	List of confirmed root causes
Assess effect of each confirmed root cause	Correlation	List of quantified effects, y = f(x) relationships

Improve Phase

The Improve phase identifies the improvements to optimize the outputs and eliminate/reduce defects and variation. It identifies x's, determines the y = f (x) relationship, and statistically validates the new process operating conditions.

IMPROVE

Step	Tools	Outputs
Identify potential solutions	Brainstorming, idea generation	List of potential solutions
Select and confirm solutions	Solution Selection, Prioritization Matrix, Force Field Analysis, Designed Experiments	Confirmed solutions
Revise process map and manage risk	Process Mapping, Failure Mode and Effects Analysis (FMEA)	Risk management plan for revised process
Prepare implementation plan	Implementation plan	Implementation plan, communication plan
Pilot solutions, check results	Piloting Solutions, PDCA	Piloted solutions and proven short-term results

Control Phase

The Control phase documents, monitors, and assigns accountability for sustaining the gains made by the process improvements.

CONTROL

Step	Tools	Outputs
Implement permanent controls	Mistake Proofing, Statistical Process Control (SPC)	Process controls
Standardize control plan	Control Plan	Control plan
Confirm improved stability and capability	SPC, Process Capability	Confirmed long-term process performance
Validate customer satisfaction and project benefits	Customer interviews, surveys, project benefits analysis	Validated customer satisfaction and project benefits
Close project	Project review and closure	Completed project documentation

ROLES AND RESPONSIBILITIES

Why is understanding roles and responsibilities important?

Prior to deployment, during deployment, and in transition to the organization, there are critical roles and responsibilities that ensure Six Sigma methodologies become ingrained in the business. Understanding who is responsible for each activity will allow for an effective deployment period and sustained performance.

Executives

- Create the vision for the Six Sigma initiative
- Define the strategic goals and measures of the organization
- Establish the business targets
- Create an environment within the organization that will promote the use of the Six Sigma methodology and tools

Senior Deployment Champion

- Is responsible for the day-to-day management of Six Sigma throughout the entire organization
- Designs the Six Sigma infrastructure and support systems (training, project approvals, human resources, reporting systems, etc.)
- Uses performance goals to get business leaders on board
- Reports to and updates the executives on the progress of deployments

- Acts as a liaison between the executives and deployment champions
- Works with deployment champions to develop a communication plan for the organization

Deployment Champion

- Is responsible for Six Sigma within his/her division or business unit
- Works with leaders of the division or business unit to determine their goals or objectives to ensure they are aligned with the executives
- Conducts a Critical To Flowdown to identify areas of opportunities that are aligned with the business goals
- Facilitates the identification and prioritization of projects
- Establishes and executes training plans
- Develops a communication plan for the division or business unit
- Reports the deployment status of the division or business unit to the senior deployment champion
- Selects the project champions
- Removes barriers for the team

Project Champion (Sponsor)

- Selects and mentors Black Belts and Green Belts
- Leads in project identification, prioritization, and defining the project scope
- Removes barriers for teams and aligns resources

- Works with deployment champions in implementing the Six Sigma infrastructure
- Communicates progress of Six Sigma projects to the deployment champion and process owners

Master Black Belt

- Is an expert on Six Sigma tools and concepts
- Trains Black Belts and ensures they are properly applying the methodology and tools
- Coaches and mentors Black Belts and Green Belts
- Maintains the training material and updates it if necessary
- Works high-level projects, many of which are across divisions or business units
- Assists champions and process owners with project selection, project management, and Six Sigma administration

Black Belt

- Is responsible for leading, executing, and completing DMAIC projects
- Teaches team members the Six Sigma methodology and tools
- Assists in identifying project opportunities and refining project details and scope
- Reports progress to project champions and process owners
- Transfers knowledge to other Black Belts and the organization
- Mentors Green Belts

Process Owner

- Is a team member
- Takes ownership of the project when it is complete
- Is responsible for maintaining the project's gains
- Removes barriers for Black Belts and Green Belts

Green Belt

- Is trained in a subset of the Six Sigma methodology and tools
- Is responsible for leading, executing, and completing smaller scope DMAIC projects, typically in his/her respective work area
- Assists Black Belts on larger scale DMAIC projects

Finance Champion

- Estimates and certifies project savings
- Establishes clear criteria on hard and soft savings
- Works with deployment champion to identify potential project opportunities
- Assigns a finance representative to each Six Sigma team

Information Technology Champion

- Ensures computer and software resourcing
- Works with Six Sigma teams to access data from existing databases
- Works with Six Sigma teams to develop an electronic project tracking system to collect, store, analyze, and report project data

- Provides training on the project tracking system
- Develops a reporting system to keep executives and project champions informed about progress in meeting goals and targets

Human Resources Champion

- Identifies roles and responsibilities for Master Black Belts, Black Belts, and Green Belts
- Works with project champions to develop a Master Black Belt, Black Belt, and Green Belt selection process
- Develops a career path transition process for Master Black Belts and Black Belts
- Works with the senior deployment champion and project champions to determine rewards and recognition for Master Black Belts, Black Belts, Green Belts, and teams

Team Member

- Participates on Six Sigma teams
- Uses own expertise to assist Black Belts and Green Belts
- Understands a subset of Six Sigma methodology and tools

Notes

GREEN BELTS

The role of a Green Belt is exciting, fun, and challenging. The role includes (1) being trained in a subset of the Six Sigma methodology and tools, (2) being responsible for leading, executing, and completing smaller scope DMAIC projects, typically in your respective work area, (3) assisting Black Belts on larger scale DMAIC projects, and (4) achieving certification as a result. This chapter is intended to explore the challenges of these four aspects and to provide some suggestions to help Green Belts succeed in their role.

Green Belt training typically includes 6-12 days of intensive classroom learning, often accompanied by online or e-learning modules. The class is often divided into two or more blocks, so that you have time to work on your project between sessions. The training is a fantastic learning opportunity and a valuable benefit, as it increases your skill set and makes you more valuable to your company. Here are some suggestions to take advantage of this experience.

- Have a project approved by your sponsor beforehand and bring a draft of the project charter with you to class. You may have an opportunity to work on aspects of the project during the class exercises, and you will be prepared to see how the tools you learn may apply to your project

- Stay involved in class and ask a lot of questions. The more questions you ask, the more you will take away from the class

- Learn about the other students' projects and think about how their experiences may be relevant to your own project

- Participate fully in the class exercises. Note what you learned during each exercise and share it with your classmates

- Try to use your new knowledge and skills as soon as possible after the class is over. Using new skills within a few weeks of class helps to make them stick

- Learn as much as you can from the instructor(s), who typically have a lot of experience with Six Sigma projects

Being responsible for leading, executing, and completing smaller scope DMAIC projects in your work area can be challenging when you have to keep up with your normal responsibilities at the same time. Here are some suggestions to help with the challenges.

- Spend some time setting expectations with your manager. You may want to get some relief from your normal responsibilities. Green Belts typically spend about 25% of their time working on their project

- Set aside specific time slots to work on your project, for example from 1:00 pm to 3:00 pm each day, or all day on Thursdays

- Some DMAIC teams have success with setting aside a block of 2-3 days to work on their project exclusively. With good planning, you may be able to work through one or more DMAIC phases in that timeframe

- Ask to have the Green Belt project included as one of your annual objectives. This helps to give it priority and visibility

- Spend some time setting expectations with your coach, including regular review meetings, communication preferences, etc. Green Belts are typically assigned to a Black Belt coach who has experience with Six Sigma projects. Take advantage of their experience and learn as much as you can from your coach

- Limit the scope of your first project as much as possible. The first project should be a learning experience. Set yourself up for success by making sure it is manageable and it can be completed within a reasonable time frame of a few months

- Network with other Green Belts or your classmates to share your project learnings

Not all Green Belts assist Black Belts on larger scale DMAIC projects. If you do get such a chance, consider these suggestions to help you take advantage of the opportunity.

- Familiarize yourself with the project as a whole, not just your part of it

- Clarify your role in the project, and set expectations with the Black Belt

- Learn how the Black Belt is approaching the project and how they use DMAIC tools

- Ask if you can shadow the Black Belt on occasion

Green Belt certification is a recognition that you have achieved a certain level of knowledge, skill, and achievement. Different organizations have different certification requirements, so spend some time familiarizing yourself with the details. Typically your knowledge level is measured by your attendance in training and a test that covers the Green Belt Body of Knowledge. Your skill level is ascertained by your coach's observations of your project activities and by a review of your project storyboard that documents the project activities (you may be required to complete one or more projects). Your achievement level is measured by the project scope, difficulty, and final results. A certification review board will typically review your project and meet with you when you have submitted evidence of your knowledge, skill, and achievement. The review board often focuses on your growth, how well you followed the methodology, how appropriately you used the tools, and to what extent you achieved the project goals. Here are a few suggestions.

- If there is a test, study for it and take it as soon as possible after the training

- Work closely with your coach to prepare for certification

- Present clear evidence of your project achievements and how you executed the project

- Follow your organization's guidelines and demonstrate how you fulfilled the certification requirements

- Celebrate and acknowledge your team members' contributions

PROJECT MANAGEMENT

Why use it?

Project management:

- Defines expected timelines and the project scope
- Focuses time and resources to meet the customer requirements for a project
- Reduces duplication of effort
- Identifies problem areas and risk
- Serves as a communication tool

What does it do?

It assigns roles, responsibilities, and timing of deliverables to allow each person to know what his or her tasks are and when they are due. It also provides the project manager with a way to monitor progress in order to take action when appropriate.

How do I do it?

There are four basic phases in project management:

1. Creating a project charter
2. Creating a project plan
3. Executing and monitoring the plan
4. Completing (closing out) the project

An in-depth discussion of the components of project management is beyond the scope of this book. For a complete description, please refer to *The Project Management Memory Jogger®*.

Project Charter

Why use it?

A project charter defines the customer needs, project scope, project goals, project success criteria, team members, and project deadlines.

How do I do it?

1. Describe the business case including a rationale for the project, identification of the customer needs from the voice of the customer analysis, linkage to upper level strategy, and an initial estimate of financials - avoid a detailed explanation of the problem and focus on the higher level importance of the issue

2. Create a problem statement that describes the gap between current and desired performance in one or two sentences and uses specific, measurable terms

3. Identify the project goals, project success criteria, and final deliverables for the project including what is to be accomplished by when, an explicit link to the problem/project statement and the primary and secondary metrics

4. Describe the project scope including the process boundaries identified in the SIPOC and what's in / what's out from the CT Trees

5. Outline the project plan including DMAIC phase target start and finish dates and any resource requirements

6. Identify the roles and responsibilities of the team members and the resource owners for project approval

Example Project Charter

1. Business Case

A strategic objective from the annual business plan is to improve customer service

One aspect of this strategy is to improve repair times for CT equipment for the 5 largest customers in North America

Initial financial forecast: reducing average repair times by 1.5 hours produces an annual savings of $550,000

2. Problem/Project Statement

The repair time for CT equipment for the 5 largest customers in North America averaged 4.5 hours in the period Jan – Dec

The benchmark in Europe for this process is 3.2 hours

3. Goal Statement

Reduce the repair time for CT equipment for the 5 largest customers in North America to install spare parts from an average of 4.5 hours to less than 3.0 hours by June

Primary metric: repair time for CT equipment, which starts when the service call is received and ends when the customer signs the repair approval document (in hours, to the nearest tenth of an hour)

Secondary metric: cost of spare parts

4. Scope

The scope includes the 5 largest customers in North America only

The process boundaries are from the start of the repair notification to the customer sign-off

5. Project Plan

Define	Feb 1 – Feb 28
Measure	Mar 1 – Mar 31
Analyze	Apr 1 – Apr 30
Improve	May 1 – May 31
Control	Jun 1 – Jun 30

Note: May need IT resources depending on solution

6. Project Team

Jill...Champion

Sue...Process owner

Jan...Team member (data collection)

Bill...Team member (process expert)

David...MBB

Kathy...BB

Project Plan

Why use it?

The project plan identifies all the work to be done, who will do the work, and when the work will get done.

How do I do it?

1. Identify the work to be done
   - Use a work breakdown structure (WBS) to identify the work to be done. The WBS is a hierarchical grouping of project tasks that organizes and defines the total project work

Work Breakdown Structure for the Development of an Educational Course

		Completion Time
Class Definition	Develop Class Objectives	2 Days
	Develop Class Outline	3 Days
	Assign Lecture Authors	1 Day
Lecture Material	Subject 1	
	First Draft	4 Days
	Review	2 Days
	Final Draft	3 Days
	Subject 2	
	First Draft	6 Days
	Review	2 Days
	Final Draft	5 Days
Printing	Hire Subcontractor	3 Days
	Print Material	5 Days

2. Assign resources and estimate the time duration

- For each task identified in the WBS, resources must be assigned and a time duration estimated. To document these activities, use an accountability matrix. The accountability matrix documents who is accountable for a particular task, whose input is required to complete a task, who is required to review the task, and who is required to sign-off on the task completion

Accountability Matrix for the Educational Course WBS

ID	Task	Duration (Days)	Tim	Alex	Julia
1	Class Definition			A	
1.1	Develop Class Objectives	2	A	R	I
1.2	Develop Class Outline	3	A	R	I
1.3	Assign Lecture Authors	1		A	
2	Lecture Material			A	
2.1	Subject 1		A		
2.1.1	First Draft	4	A		I
2.1.2	Review	2	A	R	
2.1.3	Final Draft	3	A	S	I
2.2	Subject 2				A
2.2.1	First Draft	6	I		A
2.2.2	Review	2		R	A
2.2.3	Final Draft	5	I	S	A
3	Printing			A	
3.1	Hire Subcontractor	3		A	
3.2	Print Material	5	I	A	I

Key

A	Accountable
R	Review Required
I	Input Required
S	Sign-off Required

3. **Develop a project schedule**

- Identify the critical path of the project on an Activity Network Diagram. The critical path is the shortest possible time to complete the project from the first task to the last task

Activity Network Diagram for the Educational Course Development

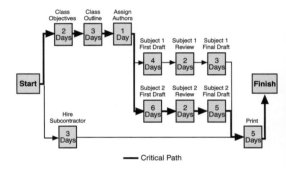

- Draw a Gantt Chart displaying the project tasks and their duration. Add appropriate milestones in the Gantt Chart

---

Team-Defined Milestones and Gantt Chart from the Educational Course Activity Network Diagram

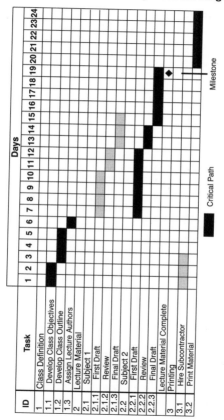

Project Execution and Monitoring

Why use it?

Once the project plan has been completed, it is time to execute the project and monitor its progress. It is important to monitor the project to ensure timely deliverables that stay within budget.

How do I do it?

1. Executing the project is doing the tasks assigned

2. Monitoring the project is done by holding regular team meetings to update the progress of the activities. At these meetings, the people accountable for each task should give a "percent complete" status of their particular task

3. Any gaps or risks in completing the program should be identified at this time and recovery plans put in place

4. An action item list for the project should be developed and the schedule should be updated to show any delays in task completion or milestone dates

Phase (Tollgate) Reviews

Why use it?

A phase (tollgate) review occurs between each phase of a DMAIC project to ensure that the intent of the project is maintained. Reviews are attended by key individuals like the champion, the Master Black Belt, Black Belts, Green Belts, and key stakeholders. Phase reviews include a presentation, discussions, and a formal approval to close each phase and move on to the next one.

What does it do?

Phase reviews answer questions like:

- Should the project continue?
- Have the phase deliverables been completed?
- Is the project on track?
- Have risks been addressed appropriately?
- What actions need to be done before the project advances?

How do I do it?

1. Set meeting dates in advance as soon as possible to ensure key members can attend

2. The project leader (Master Black Belt, Black Belt, or Green Belt) prepares a project summary (sometimes called a storyboard) to review with the group

3. Be prepared to show how each phase deliverable was completed and what was learned

4. Hold the meeting, answer the questions, issue a meeting summary, and follow up on any actions agreed to at the meeting

DMAIC Questions Managers Should Ask

Define

- Who is the customer?
- Why should we work on this project? How does it link to upper level strategy?
- What is the specific problem?
- What is the goal? What are the primary and secondary metrics?
- What is included in the scope, and what is not included?
- Who is on the project team, and what are their roles?

Measure

- Has a Y metric been established that relates back to the project charter?
- Has the Y metric been shown graphically and analyzed to help narrow down the project scope?
- Did the process map represent the actual "as is" process? Is it detailed enough to represent improvement opportunities? Can it be easily read and understood by someone unfamiliar with the process?
- What measurement system will be used? Has it passed the MSA?
- Was a capability analysis performed? Was the DPMO or Cpk value within recommended levels?

Analyze

- Have x's been identified and proven using data?
- Have hypotheses been checked using statistical methods?
- Have other MSA's been conducted where required for measuring x's?
- If a DOE was performed, what were the main effects and interactions seen to have the most effect on the output?

Improve

- How did the team arrive at the new process?

- How will the proposed changes to the process result in a real improvement in the project Y?

- What risks exist that have not been addressed through risk analysis? Are any left that are of concern to the team?

- What plan is in place to mitigate or eliminate risks? Who owns the plan?

- Have error-proofing mechanisms been discovered and what is the plan to implement them?

- Do benefits of solution(s) outweigh the cost of implementation?

- Has data from pilots confirmed that improvements have a positive effect?

- Have all stakeholders, customers, users, etc. had the project results and planned changes communicated to them?

- Does the implementation plan/action plan list what will be done, who will do it, and when it will be done? Who is managing that list?

Control

- Is there a control plan in place and has it been communicated to all who will use it? What actions will be taken if the process goes out of control?

- Has process ownership been identified and accepted?

- Have the changes made impacted any agency requirements (e.g., FDA, ISO)? Have changes been officially documented and recorded properly?

- Has an audit process been developed to ensure follow up for tracking success? Who will do the auditing?

- Are there any other items that should be done before considering this project closed?

Project Close Out

Why use it?

Formally closing out the project ensures that future teams will benefit from the documented lessons learned so that they can duplicate successes and avoid problems the team encountered.

How do I do it?

1. Hold a team meeting with the customers and stakeholders of the project to solicit feedback on opportunities for improvement and to identify things that were done well

2. Develop and document lessons learned. The team should review the results from the team meeting and its own personal experience, and document the lessons learned

3. Create a project report. The team should create a report that summarizes the team's activities on the project. The report should include all the information from the project charter, an executive summary on the project, the lessons learned on the project, a description of the final deliverable, and the customers' feedback. The report should be archived and a copy should be made available to all those involved and affected by the project

# CHANGE MANAGEMENT

Why use it?

- DMAIC projects usually entail changes that people may find difficult to understand, cope with, and sustain over time

- When change management is applied well, people are able to achieve the desired results and maintain their performance and motivation

- If change management is not applied well, DMAIC projects may fail due to people issues

What does it do?

- Change management provides support that aims to help people understand the change and equip them to improve their attitude and appropriately adjust their behavior

- It provides a consistent methodology and set of tools to help people transition from a current state to a new situation, ensuring that people feel heard, understood, recognized and respected

- Change management provides mechanisms to embed changes in systems and structures to keep people from slipping back into the old ways

Note: An in-depth discussion of the components of change management is beyond the scope of this book. Please refer to *The Team Memory Jogger®* and the many excellent books on change management.

How do I do it?

There are four basic phases in change management as it relates to DMAIC projects:

1. Preparing for change and identifying team members (done in the Define phase)

2. Managing stakeholders (started in the Define phase and continued in each subsequent DMAIC phase)

3. Managing communication (started in the Define phase and continued in each subsequent DMAIC phase)

4. Sustaining change (started in the Improve phase and completed in the Control phase)

Preparing for Change and Identifying Team Members

Why use it?

A thorough preparation for change lays the foundation for a successful project. Identifying the right team members and building teamwork helps the project advance efficiently and builds individual proficiencies.

How do I do it?

1. Create a sense of urgency by identifying what is wrong with the current situation and how it adversely affects stakeholders

2. Develop a vision of the improved future state and the benefits for stakeholders

3. Identify the roles and responsibilities of team members, along with the right people to fill those roles

4. Identify the stakeholders and resource owners who support the project, control the relevant resources, and are likely to devote sufficient attention to the project

Managing Stakeholders

Why use it?

Stakeholders have a vested interest in the project, and can either help or hinder the progress of the project depending on their perceptions of what's in it for them.

How do I do it?

1. Identify as many stakeholders as possible. Examples of stakeholders include management, process owners, suppliers, customers, process workers, subject matter experts, regulators, quality personnel, and team members

2. Determine their influence and the likelihood that they will use their power to either help or hinder the project

3. Determine their main concerns

4. Determine their current and desired level of commitment

5. Create an action plan to address their concerns and raise or maintain their commitment level

6. Make sure that key stakeholders are included in the communication plan

Example Stakeholder Management Plan

Stakeholder Management Plan

Stakeholder	Influence	Likelihood to Use Influence	Concerns	Current Commitment	Desired Commitment	Actions	Responsible Person	Date	Status
Management	High	Medium	Limited resources	Medium	High	Present vision, update weekly	Tom	Week 1	Working
Process owner	High	High	Wants results ASAP	High	High	Include on team, manage expectations	Sue	Week 1	Done
Administrators	Medium	High	Job security, work level, stress	Low	High	Include on team, communicate daily, listen to concerns	Tom	Week 2	Working
Customers	Medium	Low	Want improved delivery times	Low	Medium	Inform before any changes	Tom	Week 8	Planned

Managing Communication

Why use it?

Good communications are essential to help raise or maintain commitment levels, inform stakeholders, and keep the project moving smoothly. A communication management plan ensures that communications are relevant and effective.

How do I do it?

1. Identify key stakeholders and their concerns by completing the Stakeholder Management Plan

2. Determine the messages that need to be communicated to stakeholders

3. Determine the communication medium (written report, email, website, telephone, web meeting, face-to-face meeting, one-to-one discussion, etc.)

4. Determine the timing of the communication (when and how often)

5. Assign the responsible communicator

6. Assess the effectiveness of the communication

Example Communication Management Plan

Communication Management Plan

Stakeholder	Concerns	Messages	Medium	Timing	Responsible Person	Effectiveness	Status
Management	Limited resources	Vision and benefits Status	Face-to-face meeting, Email	Week 1 meeting, Weekly emails	Tom	Post-meeting survey, Hallway conversations	Working
Process owner	Wants results ASAP	Realistic project planning, Status	Face-to-face meeting, Weekly discussion	Week 1 meeting, Weekly discussion	Tom	One-to-one, Q&A	Working
Administrators	Job security, work level, stress	No lay-offs, Changes in work procedures, Stress management	Face-to-face meeting, Weekly discussion	Week 1 meeting, Weekly discussion	Tom	One-to-one, Q&A, Commitment	Working
Customers	Want improved delivery times	Expected changes	Email	Inform before any and all changes	Tom	Customer survey	Planned

Sustaining Change

Why use it?

There is a natural tendency for people to turn their focus to something new rather than the details of finishing the job. There need to be mechanisms in place to keep people from slipping back into the old ways. If this isn't done, people revert to the old ways, the early adopters are set up for failure, and people become cynical.

How do I do it?

1. **Inspire and motivate people by finding out what inspires key stakeholders and tailoring targeted communications accordingly:**

   • Planning for successes (even if they are not difficult) and highlighting them in communications

   • Running pilots and celebrating successes

   • Having leaders tell inspirational stories about the effects of the change

2. **Take advantage of people's tendency to copy the behavior of their role models by:**

   • Preparing leaders to ensure that they are exhibiting the right behaviors

   • Showcasing leaders and respected individuals who have adopted the change

   • Providing examples of other organizations that may have adopted the change

3. **Equip people with the knowledge and skills that they need to succeed in the new situation by:**

    - Providing training that enables people with the right knowledge and skills
    - Using coaching to support people as they learn the new ways
    - Running pilots to work out the bugs in the system and build confidence
    - Providing the right tools to make the job easier

4. **Set up systems and structures to reinforce and reward the right behaviors by:**

    - Implementing systems to measure performance and provide feedback
    - Recognizing improved performance, ensuring that bonus systems encourage the right behavior
    - Providing easily accessible support services
    - Creating an appealing physical environment

🏊 DEFINE PHASE

The purpose of the Define phase is to define the project from several perspectives, including those of the customer, the business, the process, and the major stakeholders. The major output of the Define phase is:

- An agreed-upon project charter

The project champion, with help from the project leader, should take the lead in this phase. Note that the project leader may be a Master Black Belt, a Black Belt, or a Green Belt. The champion and project leader should strive to complete as much of the Define phase as possible before the team gets too far into the details of the project.

Once the team members are assigned to the project, they assist the champion and project leader in refining the problem statement, project boundaries, and project milestones. The criteria of success for the project are agreed upon, and everything is documented in the project charter.

In the Define phase, the major tasks are to:

- Understand the Voice of the Customer (VOC)
- Assess the business benefits
- Define the problem (using Critical To Flowdown and associated tools)
- Define the process (using SIPOC)
- Define the change management strategy and select the team
- Define the project scope and approve the project charter

The chapters in this section include Voice of the Customer, Project Benefit Assessment, Critical To Flowdown, and SIPOC.

DEFINE

Step	Tools	Outputs
Understand voice of the customer (VOC)	Baseline research, interviews, focus groups, surveys	Prioritized customer needs
Assess business benefits	Project Benefit Assessment	List of project benefits
Define problem	Critical To (CT) Flowdown, IS-IS NOT analysis	Focused problem statement
Define process	SIPOC	Defined process boundaries
Define change management strategy and select team	Change Management, stakeholder management, team building	Change strategy, stakeholder strategy, communication plan, project team
Define project scope and approve charter	Project Charter	Approved project charter

Information on project charters can be found in the Project Management chapter of this book. Information on change management (including stakeholder management and communication planning) can be found in the Change Management section of this book. Information on team selection can be found in *The Team Memory Jogger®*.

VOICE OF THE CUSTOMER

Why use it?

It is important to identify the key drivers of customer satisfaction so that DMAIC projects are focused on the right issues. The term Voice of the Customer, or VOC, is used to describe customer needs and expectations. If the VOC is not understood, your project may focus on the wrong issue or deliver a result that is not desired.

What does it do?

VOC analysis identifies relevant customers and segments them according to their needs. VOC analysis provides methods to collect data from customers and then categorize that data to determine needs, wants, key issues, etc. It helps determine Critical To Quality requirements (CTQs) and focus the project on the most important measures.

How do I do it?

1. Identify both the internal and external customers of your process

2. Determine if customers can be segmented according to their needs, geography, revenue, internal/external, etc.

3. Review what information already exists and what will need to be collected

4. Determine the data collection method (baseline research, interviews, focus groups, surveys)

---

5. Collect the VOC data and categorize the information into needs, wants, expectations, key issues, etc.

6. Define CTQs in terms of customer needs and cascade these CTQs to specific measures with specifications

7. Identify which measures your project will focus on, and validate these measures with the customers and your project sponsor

Example VOC Flowdown

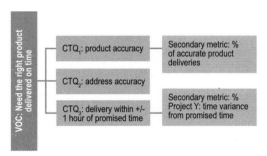

PROJECT BENEFIT ASSESSMENT

Why use it?

Project benefit assessment helps to determine the value of the DMAIC project to the business. The objective is to determine, in an economically correct way, what estimated benefits will be delivered by the project and when they will appear. Project benefit assessment can help compare projects, build project portfolios, and track the benefits of a Six Sigma program.

What does it do?

In the Define phase, project benefit assessment is used to estimate the potential benefits of the project. In the Improve phase, it is used as an input to cost-benefit analysis of proposed solutions. In the Control phase, the actual benefits from the project are calculated and compared to the original estimate.

How do I do it?

1. Contact the Six Sigma financial representatives and include them in financial discussions. Note that each company has different rules governing the accounting of project benefits, and it is important to consult with a financial expert in these matters

2. In the Define phase, estimate the project benefits that would result from achieving the project objective

Project Benefits			
Hard		**Soft**	
Revenue Enhancement and Cost Reduction	Working Capital Reduction	Cost Avoidance	Non-financial Benefits

3. Categorize the benefits as:

   - Hard (visible in financial accounts)
   - Soft (not visible in financial accounts but still valuable to the company)

4. Sub-categorize the benefits in the Hard category as:

   - Revenue enhancement (e.g., higher sales) or cost reduction (e.g., higher quality, reduced waste, or higher efficiency)
   - Working capital reduction (e.g., reduced inventories)

5. Sub-categorize the benefits in the Soft category as:

   - Cost avoidance (e.g., regulatory compliance or reducing need for additional resources to meet increased demand)
   - Non-financial benefits (e.g., customer satisfaction, employee engagement, or sustainability enhancements)

6. In the Improve phase, conduct a cost-benefit analysis of the proposed solutions to help select the best solutions

7. In the Control phase, validate the project benefits that were actually achieved and compare them to the estimates made in the Define phase

# CRITICAL TO FLOWDOWN

Why use it?

During the Define phase, project champions and project leaders (Master Black Belts, Black Belts, Green Belts) use Critical To Trees (CT Trees) and Critical To Matrices (CT Matrices) as tools to define DMAIC projects. The CT Tree helps ensure that what the organization is working on is critical to its business and its customers and strikes a balance between both. The CT Matrix identifies customer requirements and links these requirements in a matrix fashion to those organizational processes most likely to affect them. (Both of these tools consider customers to be either the external or internal users of the product or service.)

What does it do?

The CT Tree translates needs considered vital by the customer into product and service characteristics and links these characteristics to organizational processes. The CT Matrix is a simplified version of a Quality Function Deployment (QFD). A single DMAIC project could employ CT Trees and CT Matrices at various levels within a process.

Before creating a CT Tree or CT Matrix, certain terms to describe characteristics in these tools must be defined:

- *Critical To Satisfaction* (CTS) characteristics relate specifically to the satisfaction of the customer. The customer will typically define satisfaction in one of four ways:

  1. *Critical To Quality* (CTQ) characteristics are product, service, and/or transactional characteristics that significantly influence one or more CTSs in terms of quality

2. *Critical To Delivery* (CTD) characteristics are product, service, and/or transactional characteristics that significantly influence one or more CTSs in terms of delivery (or cycle)

3. *Critical To Cost* (CTC) characteristics are product, service, and/or transactional characteristics that significantly influence one or more CTSs in terms of cost

4. *Critical to the Process* (CTP) characteristics are process parameters that significantly influence a CTQ, CTD, and/or CTC

For the equation $y = f(x_1, x_2, \ldots x_n)$, the CTQ, CTD, or CTC characteristics represent the dependent variable (y), and the CTP characteristics represent the independent variables (x's).

The CTQ, CTD, and CTC are "opportunities for nonconformance" that must be measured and reported, while the CTP represents "control opportunities."

How do I do it?

There are two types of trees or flowdowns that need to be created to strike a balance between the business and the customer: *process trees* and *product trees*.

- A *process tree* is a breakdown of the organization's engineering, manufacturing, service, and transaction processes. CTPs are identified at the lowest level of this tree

- A *product tree* is a hierarchical breakdown of the organization's product or service, which allows a visualization of the CTQ, CTD, and CTC characteristics at each level of the hierarchy

A typical CTX product tree is shown in the following figure. The numbers in the text that follows correspond to the numbers in circles in the graphic.

CTX Product Tree or Flowdown

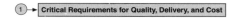

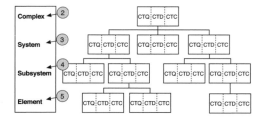

1. Critical requirements for quality, delivery, and cost are translated from the CTS characteristics

2. The complex level is the first level of the product tree and describes the final product or service that is delivered to the customer. CTQs, CTDs, and CTCs can be found at this level and are usually expressed as a function of the immediate lower level characteristics: CTQ-complex = f (CTQ-system$_1$, ... CTQ-system$_n$)

3. The system level is a more detailed breakdown of the complex level. CTQs, CTDs, and CTCs can be found at this level and are usually expressed as a function of the immediate lower level characteristics: CTQ-system = f (CTQ-subsystem$_1$, ... CTQ-subsystem$_n$)

4. The subsystem level is a more detailed breakdown of the system level. CTQs, CTDs, and CTCs can be found at this level and are usually expressed as a function of the immediate lower level characteristics: CTQ-system = f (CTQ-element$_1$, ... CTQ-element$_n$)

5. The element level is the lowest level of the tree. Its components are not divisible. CTQs, CTDs, and CTCs can be found at this level

The size of the tree is dependent on the complexity of the product or service (e.g., a spark plug is less complex than a car and would therefore have a less complex CT Tree). Described in the following figure is a tree that looks at the product a business might sell to a customer.

Product Flowdown

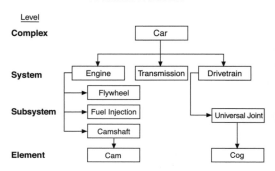

A given product or service at any level of the hierarchy in this tree can have quality, delivery, and/or cost issues that concern customers. Within the hierarchy, the organization must consider whether it is satisfying those customer needs.

A CTX Process Tree for the major processes that support the engineering, manufacturing, marketing, and sales of this car can also be created, as described in the figure on the next page.

Process Flowdown

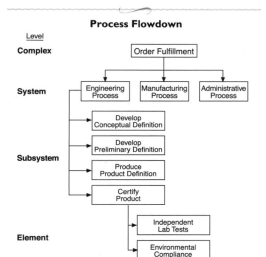

Level

Complex

Order Fulfillment

System

Engineering Process

Manufacturing Process

Administrative Process

Subsystem

Develop Conceptual Definition

Develop Preliminary Definition

Produce Product Definition

Certify Product

Element

Independent Lab Tests

Environmental Compliance

This process tree will help identify the individual x's that can potentially impact the individual y's of a product.

To determine which product and/or process needs the most attention the organization will create a CT Matrix. The CT Matrix, like the CT Tree, is developed by the project champion and the project leader, together with a team that collectively has process/product knowledge and, to the greatest extent possible, an understanding of the voice of the customer. It is owned by the product or process owner.

Once the product tree has been developed and customer requirements (CTS) identified, the organization can use a CT Matrix to determine which processes are most likely to impact those CTS requirements, as shown in the figure on the next page.

Example CT Matrix

Process Tree / Subsystem Level — Product Tree / Complex Level	Needs to achieve 35 mpg highway 27 mpg city	Needs to hold six occupants comfortably	Needs to convert to all-wheel drive on the fly	Needs to cost under $40K	Must be available July	Must have superior exterior finishing
Engineering System						
· Develop conceptual definition	✔	✔	✔	✔	✔	✔
· Develop preliminary definition	✔	✔	✔	✔	✔	✔
· Produce product definition	✔	✔	✔	✔	✔	✔
· Certify product	✔				✔	
· Support product development						
· Manage project					✔	
Manufacturing System						
· Bid preparation						
· Program or contract start-up						
· Technical data preparation						
· Projection of first and subs	✔			✔	✔	✔
· Testing and commissioning					✔	
Customer Support						
· Product management						
· Manage customer						
· Contracts						
· Spares/tech pub/training				✔	✔	
· Maintenance engineering						
· Completion center				✔	✔	✔
· Aviation service						
Administrative Process						
· Finance/budget/billing						
· Human resources relations						
· Strategic plan and communication						

In this example matrix, it appears that the greatest area for opportunity to effect change is in the Engineering System. The team could then collect more detailed information about the individual cells within this matrix to help narrow the focus.

No matter the complexity of the product or process, these top-level tools assist the project champion and project leader in continually narrowing the focus. More detailed information about the individual cells within the matrix could be collected until the project is scoped to a manageable level. High-level process maps are created, followed by more detailed process maps as the input variables become more key and additional granularity is required. (Process mapping is explained in more detail in a subsequent chapter in this book.)

Tip
An important concept to remember is to avoid "drilling down" too quickly into the details of the process and stay at the highest process level possible for as long as possible.

At this point, the project leader still needs to determine where the greatest opportunity for improvement is in the process, by collecting more data about the individual process steps. Subsequently, the project leader will need to create a Cause & Effect (C&E) Matrix (also known as a Prioritization Matrix), as shown in the following figure. The numbers in the graphic correspond to the steps required to complete this matrix.

C&E Matrix

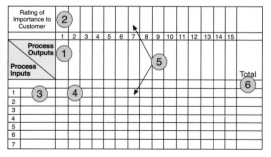

To complete this matrix:

1. The y's from the process identified from the previous CT Matrix are placed across the columns of the C&E Matrix

2. The y's are ranked relative to one another on a scale of 1-10 with respect to their importance to the customer

3. The process steps or CTXs obtained from the process mapping exercise are placed down the first column of the matrix, establishing the identity of each row. Depending on the number of process inputs, starting at a higher level (of process steps) is much more efficient

4. The steps or CTXs are compared to the y's of the process by a force-ranking on the following (or similar) scale: 0, 1, 4, and 9. The forced ranking is done to prioritize the CTXs. In this step, the team should ask, "If a particular x was changed, would it significantly impact y, either positively or negatively?" If the team considers that the impact would be significant, then a ranking of 9 is given. If the team does not think the y will be impacted, then a score of 0 or 1 will be appropriate. If one person wants to give a ranking of 9 and the other team members want to give a ranking of 1, the team should not take the average, but should discuss the situation to determine what knowledge the person who wants to rank a 9 has that the other team members do not have

5. For each row, the sum-product is calculated by multiplying the cell rating (from step 4) by the importance rating for the y in that column (from step 2). The products across each row are added together and stored in the last column, titled Total (6)

6. The Totals column is then sorted in descending order. The values with the highest totals are those CTXs that are most likely to impact the project

Example C&E Matrix:

A project leader was assigned to a team with the Engineering Systems process owners/representatives. Their goal was to apply the C&E Matrix to determine the initial "process" focus of a DMAIC project within the larger Engineering Systems process. To ensure that the team was cross-functional, the product development and management teams from each facet of the organization were also represented. The team started with previously created CT Trees and a CT Matrix. Each member had also conducted a review of the new product under development and reviewed data collected on previous new product introductions in their respective areas. They decided to create a C&E Matrix based on the current process performance and the relationship between customer requirements of this particular product and the Engineering Systems process steps.

The Team's C&E Matrix

Rating of Importance to Customer	6	9	9	10	10	7	
	1	2	3	4	5	6	
Process Inputs (Steps)	Needs to achieve 35 mpg highway 27 mpg city	Needs to hold six occupants comfortably	Needs to convert to all-wheel drive on the fly	Needs to cost under $40K	Must be available July	Must have superior exterior finish	Total
2 Preliminary Design (D)	9	9	9	9	9	④	424
3 Product Definition - Optimize (O)	9	4	9	9	4	4	329
6 Manage Project	4	1	4	⑨	⑨	4	277
5 Support Production Development	4	4	4	4	1	⑨	209
1 Conceptual - Identify (I)	1	4	4	1	9	4	206
4 Certify Product - Validate (V)	4	1	4	4	4	1	156
Total Column Score	186	207	306	360	360	182	

CTSs were taken from the CT Matrix and placed along the top of the C&E Matrix. All six of these CTSs were then assigned a ranked score or rating from 1 to 10, based on the importance to the customer. The team noticed that these importance ratings received rankings from 6 through 10. The CT Matrix also identified the major process steps, 1 through 6, of the Engineering Systems process. (This served as their high-level process map.) These process steps then served as the process inputs down the left side of the matrix. Each step was ranked on the 0,1,4,9 scale to ascertain the linkage between the Voice of the Process (VOP), the process steps, and the Voice of the Customer (VOC) or CTSs. (The VOP are the "causes" and the VOC is the "effect"; hence the "Cause & Effect" Matrix.)

(To narrow the focus, another C&E Matrix was then created to link the customer requirements to the process steps. This is a mid-level application of the C&E Matrix because it is dealing with process steps vs. more-detailed process inputs from each step. Subsequent C&E Matrices can be created after one particular process or area is highlighted as having the greatest impact on the customer requirements.)

The team assessed the linkages based on collective experience and data. Considerations were based on existing and proposed process capability and technology roadmaps. For example, the "Preliminary Design Efforts" were scored lower (4) for "superior exterior finish" because this was an existing capability for the organization. The team was more concerned with maintaining exterior finish in the production process and therefore assigned a score of 9 to "Support Production Development." Also, the management team was much more concerned with managing total cost and schedule as it pertained to the "Manage Project" process step. Upon completion of the rankings, the totals were calculated and the steps were sorted in descending order of the total scores.

A Pareto Chart was created based on the total scores for each process step, showing that the Preliminary Design step was considered to be the most critical step in the process, because it related to all of the customer requirements identified on the matrix. This process step contributes 26.5% of the total variation or risk to the development of this new product. Therefore, the first DMAIC project to be defined should concentrate efforts in this area.

Pareto Chart
of the C&E Matrix Results

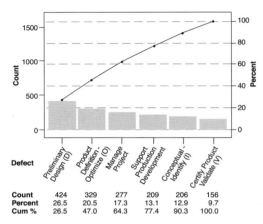

Defect	Preliminary Design (D)	Product Definition - Optimize (O)	Manage Project	Support Production Development	Conceptual - Identify (I)	Certify Product Validate (V)
Count	424	329	277	209	206	156
Percent	26.5	20.5	17.3	13.1	12.9	9.7
Cum %	26.5	47.0	64.3	77.4	90.3	100.0

A recommended cross-validation is to evaluate the total column scores in the matrix for each customer requirement. These scores are calculated similarly to the row totals. The column scores represent the weighted sums of the CTSs as they relate to the entire Engineering Systems process. Comparing these totals to the ratings assigned to their respective CTS ensures that the process gives fair weight and consideration to each of the customer requirements relative to the assigned ratings. A discrepancy would indicate either a significant disconnect in the process, unrealistic rankings of the process steps, or missing steps not included in the matrix. As an extreme example, a column totaling zero would indicate that none of the listed CTXs had any perceived effect on the CTY of that column.

Links to Other Tools

The team's next step would be to create a more detailed process map of the Preliminary Design process. The process map will include inputs and outputs of each detailed step. A subsequent C&E Matrix can then be conducted on the detailed process steps or process inputs from the detailed process map. The team will then evaluate the process inputs associated with these steps on an FMEA. The FMEA will be completed with the comprehensive list of inputs.

Each tool is applied with greater granularity until the potential critical inputs or x's are identified. The results of the C&E Matrix exercise are used in the FMEA exercise. The team will strategically "drill down" into the various levels of the process, from the complex level down to the element level. The CTXs that are identified as having high values in the CT Matrix are the potential critical x's. Data should be collected around these x's to validate their significance.

The process output variables from the C&E Matrix should drive additional action to complete capability studies on the y's, including measurement system analysis. (Measurement systems analysis is discussed in greater detail in a subsequent chapter of this book.) For every input that has a high impact on the CTYs of interest on the C&E Matrix and/or FMEA, an initial control plan could be developed; subsequent action on capabilities on the x's may be postponed until the completion of the FMEA.

Links to Other Tools

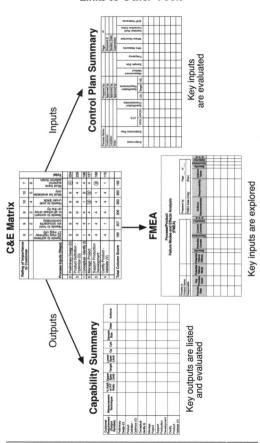

C&E Matrix

Rating of Importance to Customer	6	9	9	9	10	7	Total
Process Inputs (Steps)	Needs to achieve 200 mpg highway / 100 mpg city	Must have superior comfortability	Needs to hold six occupants	Must be available July	Needs to cost under $40k	Needs to convert to exterior travel on the fly	
1 Preliminary Design (D)	9	9	9	4	9	(4)	334
2 Product Definition - Optimize (O)	9	9	4	9	9	4	239
3 Conceptual - Identify (I)	9	4	9	9	4	4	196
4 Manage Project	4	1	4	(9)	(9)	4	187
5 Support Production Development	4	4	9	4	1	4	169
6 Certify Product - Validate (V)	4	1	4	4	4	4	116
Total Column Score	186	207	306	360	360	182	

Inputs →

Control Plan Summary

Key inputs are evaluated

FMEA →

Process/Product Failure Modes and Effects Analysis (FMEA)

Key inputs are explored

Outputs →

Capability Summary

Key outputs are listed and evaluated

 SIPOC

Why use it?

In the Define phase, a SIPOC—which stands for Suppliers, Inputs, Processes, Outputs, Customers—helps to focus the scope of a DMAIC project from the process perspective.

- It helps teams identify the process elements that are relevant to the project. Process elements, such as:
    - Suppliers who supply the inputs to the process
    - Inputs that are required to produce the outputs
    - Process steps at a high level
    - Outputs from the process
    - Customers who receive an output from this process
- It helps stakeholders understand the process boundaries
- It provides a high-level understanding of the process
- It identifies the specific start and stop points of the process to help prevent scope creep
- It serves as the starting point for creating a more detailed process map that will be made in the Measure phase

What does it do?

A SIPOC provides a high-level overview of the as-is process under investigation. It helps teams define the specific process elements that are within the scope of the project, as well as helping teams to stay broad enough to encompass all the process steps and inputs that may help them identify potential root causes, but narrow enough to be manageable.

How do I do it?

1. Name the process
2. Identify the start and stop points
3. Identify 3–7 high-level process steps
4. List the measurable outputs of process
5. List the customers who receive outputs
6. List the measurable inputs of process
7. List the suppliers who supply inputs

Tip Stay at a high level as there is no need for fine details yet.

Tip Pay attention to the start and stop points of the process.

Tip Ensure that the scope is broad enough to encompass the issues, yet narrow enough to be manageable. The SIPOC can be an input to the scope section of your project charter.

Tip Review the SIPOC with your team to ensure that everyone is on the same page.

Tip Confirm that the suppliers and customers are included on the initial list of stakeholders.

SIPOC Template

Suppliers	Inputs	Process	Outputs	Customers
Supplier companies	Customer requirements	Start (what triggers the process steps)	Products	External customers
Departments	Materials, components, parts	Step 1	Components	Internal customers
Individuals	Data	Step 2	Parts	Users of the outputs
Processes	Schedules	...	Data	Companies
	Procedures	Step n	Reports	Departments
	Equipment	Stop (what signals the end of the process)	Records	Individuals
	Infrastructure		Key performance indicators	Processes
	Software		Schedules	
	Systems			

Example SIPOC for Medical Equipment Sales Process

Suppliers	Inputs	Process	Outputs	Customers
Account managers	Sales leads	Study information related to sales lead	Booked order	Hospital buyers
Regional managers	Product information	Make appointment	Client information	Radiologists
Marketing	Demo site schedule	Meet with client	Product information	Order processing department
Engineering		Schedule demo	Price	Logistics
Demo site		Demonstrate products	Delivery schedule	Manufacturing
		Present quotation		
		Book order		

MEASURE PHASE

The purpose of the Measure phase is to document the as-is process and to measure the baseline process performance as it relates to the customer needs identified in the Define phase. The major deliverables include:

- A detailed process map
- A data collection plan with an operational definition of the project Y
- A measurement systems analysis
- A process performance analysis
- A risk management plan
- A reconfirmed project charter

When the Measure phase is complete, the team has enough understanding of the process and the performance gap to start looking for root causes in the Analyze phase.

In the Measure phase, the major tasks are to:

- Map the as-is process and look for quick wins
- Prepare a data collection plan focusing on the project Y
- Anaiyze the measurement systems to ensure that the data are accurate and precise
- Analyze the data to determine process performance in terms of stability and capability
- Manage risk and reconfirm the project charter

MEASURE

Step	Tools	Outputs
Map as-is process and look for quick wins	Process Mapping, value stream map	Process map
Prepare data collection plan	Data Collection template	Data collection plan
Analyze measurement system	Gauge calibration, Gauge R&R studies	Validated measurement systems
Analyze process stability and capability	Time series plot, Process Capability studies	Process performance metrics
Manage risk and reconfirm charter	Risk Assessment and Management, Project Charter	Risk management plan, reconfirmed charter

The chapters in this section include Process Mapping, Data Collection Plan, Basic Statistics and Variation, Measurement Systems Analysis, Rolled Throughput Yield, Sigma Values, Process Capability, and Risk Assessment and Management.

 # PROCESS MAPPING

Why use it?

Process mapping identifies the flow of events in a process as well as the inputs (x's) and outputs (y's) in each step of a process. The DMAIC team may decide to use a simple process map, a cross-functional deployment flow diagram, or a value stream map to help visualize and understand the process.

What does it do?

Process mapping:

- Graphically identifies the steps in a process

- Visually shows the complexity of a process and identifies sources of non-value-added activities (i.e., rework loops and redundancy in a process)

- Identifies the key process input variables (x's) that go into a process step and the resultant key output variables (y's)

- Classifies all input variables (x's) to a process step as noise, controllable factors, or standard operating procedures (SOPs)

Process maps can be used to

- Review the process with the team to ensure everyone is on the same page

- Check for areas where it may be useful to collect data

- Look for obvious disconnects, non-value-added steps, and quick wins

- Help generate a list of potential root causes in the Analyze phase

- Start from the as-is process as a basis for the to-be process in the Improve phase

Components of a Process Map

- The inputs (x's) are the key process variables that are required to perform a process step. Inputs could be anything in the categories of people, methods, materials, machinery, measurements, or environment
- The process steps are the tasks that transform the inputs of the process into the outputs of the process
- The outputs (y's) are the key variables resulting from the performance of the process step. Outputs can be goods, services, measurements, or consequences

Process Map

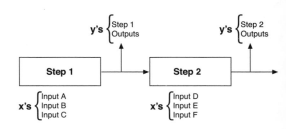

How do I do it?

1. Define the scope of the process (use the SIPOC from the Define phase as the basis for this step)

   • Clearly define where the process starts and stops. These are the process boundaries

   • Process maps can be done at different levels, such as an overall level, operation level, or micro-task level. The team should decide which level is appropriate. An overall level may be appropriate for general audiences to gain an overall view of the process, while a more detailed level may be appropriate when looking for root causes

2. Document all the steps in the process

   • To do this correctly, "walk through" the process by pretending to be the product or service being operated on. Document all the steps of the as-is process, not the should-be process. Activities are shown as a rectangle on a process map

   • Document the decision points. Decision points must pose a question. The response to the question will lead to multiple paths. Decision points are shown as a diamond on a process map

3. List all outputs (y's) at each process step

4. List all inputs (x's) at each process step

5. Classify all inputs (x's) as:

   • Controllable (C): Inputs that can be changed to affect the output (y). Examples are speed or feed rate on a machine, temperature or pressure in a thermodynamic process, or document type or batch size in a transactional process

---

- Standard operating procedures (S): Standard methods or procedures for running the process. Examples are cleaning, safety, loading of components in an industrial process, training, calling method, or data entry items in a transactional process

- Noise (N): Things that cannot or that have been chosen not to be controlled due to cost or difficulty. Examples are ambient temperature or humidity in an industrial process, computer network, or operator experience in a transactional process

6. As applicable, list the operating specification and process targets for controllable inputs

- For the controllable inputs that have these targets, list the target input and the specified lower and/or upper limits on the setting

Class Lecture Development Process Map

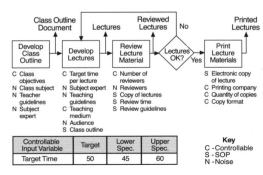

Controllable Input Variable	Target	Lower Spec.	Upper Spec.
Target Time	50	45	60

Key
C - Controllable
S - SOP
N - Noise

Cross-functional Deployment Flow Diagram (Swim Lane Diagram)

Why use it?

When a process spans several departments it is helpful to visualize where the handoffs occur, because problems often occur at departmental boundaries.

What does it do?

The process map depicts each step in the process, as well as:

- Inputs to each step
- Outputs of each step
- Times of each step
- Which function/department performs the step

How do I do it?

Identify the project scope and start/stop points of the process (from the SIPOC)

1. Walk the process

2. Determine the type of process map to use

3. Document all tasks or operations needed in the production of a product or service

4. Locate any documentation that describes how each task is executed

5. Map the tasks to show the as-is flow from left to right

6. Use paper and pencil or sticky notes on a large wall area to draft the first version

---

Cross-Functional Deployment Flow Diagram

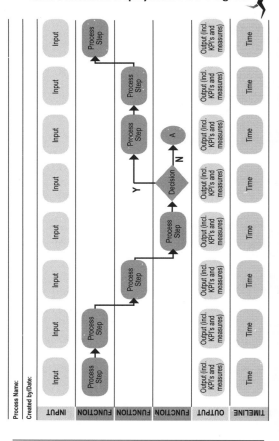

Process Name:

Created by/Date:

© 2018 GOAL/QPC

# Value Stream Map (VSM)

Why use it?

Value stream maps are used to identify long-term improvement opportunities to reduce lead time and waste. They help teams to identify high-level problem areas, map the current state and quick-win opportunities, map the future state to increase speed and eliminate waste, and to plan for long-term improvements.

What does it do?

A VSM depicts the flow of materials and information. It identifies:

- Process steps
- Waste
- Lead times
- How flow is driven
- Performance measures, such as cycle time, wait time, inventory, work in process, defect rates
- Opportunities for improvement

How do I do it?

1. Decide on product family and level of detail
2. Assemble the mapping team and materials
3. Walk the process
4. Record what you see and hear from the operators, including details of each step
5. Order the major material flow process steps

---

6. Identify rework loops

7. Identify direction and format of information/ material flow with arrows

8. Insert relevant metric data (cycle time, changeover time, etc.) in appropriate steps or sub-steps

9. Identify inventory and Work-In-Process (WIP) areas, along with quantities and wait times

10. Insert total cycle times and wait times at the bottom of the chart

VSM example

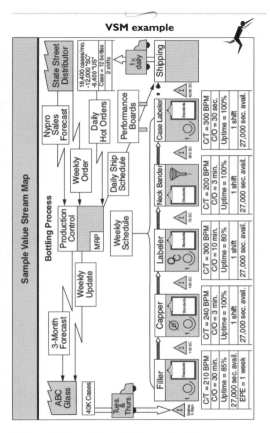

Sample Value Stream Map

Refer to *The Lean Enterprise Memory Jogger®* for more information on value stream mapping.

Notes

DATA COLLECTION PLAN

Why use it?

Collecting data is necessary to make good decisions in DMAIC projects. Data collection plans help ensure that the DMAIC team collects the right data and that it is collected the right way. Data collection plans include operational definitions which provide everyone with the same meaning in terms of the scope of the measure (what is included and what is not included) and the measurement process (ensuring consistency and reliability).

What does it do?

A data collection plan is a one-page document that describes the what, where, when, who, and how of collecting data for a project. An operational definition is a concise description of a relevant measure. It describes:

- The specific criteria used for the measure (the what)

- The methodology used to obtain the measure (the how)

How do I do it?

1. Determine which data to collect (including the type of measure)

2. Create an operational definition (including the what and the how)

   - Describe precisely what the metric represents:

     - What is included

     - What is excluded

     - Units and resolution

- Describe how the metric is measured:
    - Triggers
    - Physical measurements
    - Calculations
    - Data storage
    - Reporting

3. If available, include information on specification limits, measurement system precision, and capability

4. Identify who is responsible for collecting the data

5. Determine frequency and timing of the data collection

6. Determine sample size and subgroups

7. Determine where the data is stored

8. Create the data collection form

9. Communicate with the relevant people, and review the status of the data collection plan periodically

Example Data Collection Plan

| Project Leader | Jane |
| Project Name | Sales lead time reduction |

What does the data represent and how is it measured?								Sampling plan					
Metric (units)	Type of measure (Output Y, Input X, Process X)	Controllable (C) - Noise (N)	Operational definition	Measurement system	Lower spec limit	Upper spec limit	Who is responsible?	Frequency (how often is data collected?)	Sample size?	If subgrouping, what does a subgroup represent?	Where is the data stored?	How is the data reported?
Sales lead time (days)	Y	NA	The time in days (to the nearest day) from the date a sales lead for CT equipment is entered into SAP to the date a sale for the equipment is recorded in the same system. Sales not recorded within 6 months are not included in this metric.	SAP (passed gauge R&R study on 02-04)	NA	30 days	All sales reps enter their own data. Bill reports the data.	Sales reps enter the data daily. Bill reports the data weekly.	Weekly sample size varies from 25 - 50 units.	Weekly data	SAP	A control chart is generated on a weekly basis and reported in the Sales intranet site.

Notes

BASIC STATISTICS AND VARIATION

Why use it?

Once facts or data have been classified and summarized, they must be interpreted, presented, or communicated in an efficient manner to drive data-based decisions. Statistical problem-solving methods are used to determine if processes are on target, if the total variability is small compared to specifications, and if the process is stable over time. Businesses can no longer afford to make decisions based on averages alone; process variations and their sources must be identified and eliminated.

What does it do?

The Measure phase involves designing data collection plans, collecting data, and then using that data to describe the process.

Descriptive statistics are used to describe or summarize a specific collection of data (typically samples of data). Descriptive statistics encompass both numerical and graphical techniques, and are used to determine the:

- Central tendency of the data
- Spread or dispersion of the data
- Symmetry and skewness of the data

Inferential statistics is the method of collecting samples of data and making inferences about population parameters from the sample data.

Before reviewing basic statistics, the different types of data must be identified. The type of data that has been collected as process inputs (x's) and/or outputs (y's) will determine the type of statistics or analysis that can be performed.

Selecting Statistical Techniques

Outputs

		Attribute	Variable
Inputs	Attribute	Proportion tests, Chi-square	t-test, ANOVA, DOE, Regression
	Variable	Discriminant analysis, Logistic regression	Correlation, Multiple regression

The two classifications of data types are continuous (variable), or attribute (discrete).

Continuous data:

- Has no boundaries between adjoining values
- Includes most non-counting intervals and ratios (e.g., time)

Attribute data:

- Has clear boundaries
- Includes nominals, counts, and rank-orders (e.g., Monday vs. Friday, an electrical circuit with or without a short)

Data Type Classifications

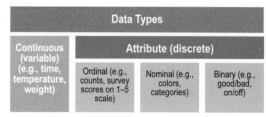

© 2018 GOAL/QPC

Tip It is more informative to collect continuous data to enable straightforward descriptive and inferential statistics. In the Data Type Classifications graphic, the data types are arranged from left to right in terms of most resolution to least resolution (continuous, ordinal, nominal, binary).

How do I do it?

Measures of Central Tendency

There are three measures of central tendency: the mean, the median, and the mode.

1. The *mean* (μ) is the average of a set of values. It can be strongly influenced by extreme values. The mean of a population can be calculated using the formula:

$$\mu = \sum_{i=1}^{N} x_i = \frac{x_1 + x_2 + x_3 + \ldots + x_N}{N}$$

   N = total number of data points in the population

$$\sum_{i=1}^{N} = \text{Sum of all values from the first to last}$$

   Examples:

   Average Days Late: $\dfrac{1 + 2 + 3 + 4 + 5}{5} = 3.0$

   Inspection (Pass/Fail): $\dfrac{0 + 0 + 1 + 1}{4} = 0.5$

2. The *median* is the midpoint in a string of sorted data, where 50% of the observations or values are below and 50% are above. If there are an even number of observations, it is the average of the two middle numbers. The median is less sensitive to extreme values than the mean

Tip Order the data from low to high values when determining the median. This will make it easier to select the middle observation.

Examples:

For the odd number of observations 1, 2, 3, 4, 5, 6, 7, the median is 4

For the even number of observations 1, 2, 3, 4, 5, 6, 7, 8, the median is 4.5

3. The *mode* is the most frequently occurring value in a data set. For example, in the data set 1, 2, 3, 3, 5, 7, 9, the mode is 3

Measures of Spread

Measures of spread include the range, the deviation, the variance, and the standard deviation.

1. The *range* is the difference between the largest and smallest observations in a data set

   Range = maximum observation – minimum observation

   For the data set 1,2,3,3,5,7,9, the range is 9-1 = 8.

2. The *deviation* is the distance between a data point and the mean

   Deviation = $(X-\mu)$

   In the example 1,2,3,3,5,7,9, the mean is (1+2+3+3+5+7+9)/7 = 30/7 = 4.29, and the deviation of the data point 9 is (9 - 4.29) = 4.71

3. The *variance* is the average squared deviation about the mean. The squared deviation of a single point is calculated by subtracting it from the mean and squaring the difference

4. The *standard deviation* is the square root of the average squared deviation about the mean (i.e., the square root of the variance). The standard deviation is the most commonly used measurement to quantify variability and will be in the same units as the data collected. The formula to calculate the standard deviation in a population is:

$$\sigma = \sqrt{\dfrac{\sum\limits_{i=1}^{N}(x_i - \mu)^2}{N}}$$

To determine the population standard deviation for the data set 1, 2, 3:

X	μ	X − μ	(X − μ)²
1	2	− 1	1
2	2	0	0
3	2	1	1
Σ = 6			2
N = 3			
μ = 2			

$$\sigma = \sqrt{\dfrac{\sum\limits_{i=1}^{N}(x_i - \mu)^2}{N}}$$

$$\sigma = \sqrt{\dfrac{(1-2)^2 + (2-2)^2 + (3-2)^2}{3}}$$

$$\sigma = \sqrt{0.667} = 0.8167$$

The variance for a sum of two independent variables is found by adding both variances. The standard deviation for the total is the square root of the sum of both variances.

If σ_1^2 = variance of variable 1, and

σ_2^2 = variance of variable 2, then

$\sigma_T^2 = \sigma_1^2 + \sigma_2^2$ and

$\sigma_T = \sqrt{\sigma_1^2 + \sigma_2^2}$

Population vs. Sample

A population is every possible observation or census, but it is very rare to capture the entire population in data collection. Instead, samples, or subsets of populations as illustrated in the following figure, are captured.

Populations and Samples

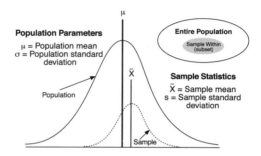

A statistic, by definition, is a number that describes a sample characteristic. Information from samples can be used to "infer" or approximate a population characteristic called a parameter. (More information about using samples to infer population parameters can be found in the chapter on Confidence Intervals in this book.)

Sample Statistics Approximate
the Population Parameters

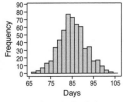

Sample Statistics

$\bar{X}$ = 84.99
s^2 = 34.57
s = 5.88
n = 600

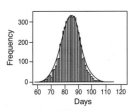

Population Parameters

μ = 85.06
σ^2 = 36.53
σ = 6.04
N = 5,000

Data is obtained using samples because the entire population may not be known or may be too expensive to measure. Descriptive statistics can apply to any sample or population; however, the equations are unique for each.

Population and Sample Equations

Sample mean
n = A subset of the population

$$\bar{X} = \sum_{i=1}^{n} x_i = \frac{x_1 + x_2 + x_3 + \ldots + x_n}{n}$$

Sample standard deviation

$$s = \sqrt{\frac{\sum_{i=1}^{n}(x_i - \bar{x})^2}{(n-1)}}$$

Population mean
N = Every member of the population

$$\mu = \sum_{i=1}^{N} x_i = \frac{x_1 + x_2 + x_3 + \ldots + x_N}{N}$$

Population standard deviation

$$\sigma = \sqrt{\frac{\sum_{i=1}^{N}(x_i - \mu)^2}{N}}$$

Properties of a Normal Distribution

A normal distribution can be described by its mean and standard deviation. The standard normal distribution is a special case of the normal distribution and has a mean of zero and a standard deviation of one. The tails of the distribution extend to ± infinity. The area under the curve represents 100% of the possible observations. The curve is symmetrical such that each side of the mean has the same shape and contains 50% of the total area. Theoretically, about 95% of the population is contained within ± 2 standard deviations.

The Standard Normal Curve

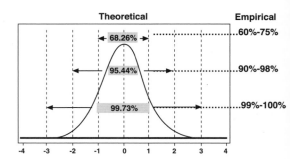

If a data set is normally distributed, then the standard deviation and mean can be used to determine the percentage (or probability) of observations within a selected range. Any normally distributed scale can be transformed to its equivalent Z scale or score using the formula:

$$Z = (x-\mu)/\sigma$$

x will often represent a lower specification limit (LSL) or upper specification limit (USL). Z, the "sigma value," is a measure of standard deviations from the mean.

Any normal data distribution can be transformed to a standard normal curve using the Z transformation. The area under the curve is used to predict the probability of an event occurring.

Z Transformations

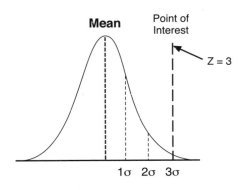

Example:

If the mean is 85 days and the standard deviation is five days, what would be the yield if the USL is 90 days?

Using The Z-Transform To Predict Yield

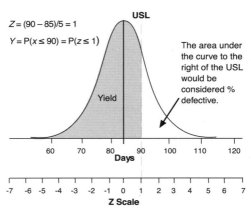

$Z = (90 - 85)/5 = 1$

$Y = P(x \le 90) = P(z \le 1)$

The area under the curve to the right of the USL would be considered % defective.

Yield

Days

Z Scale

$P(z < 1) = 1 - P(z > 1) = 1 - 0.15865 = 0.8413 \; \text{Yield} \cong 84.1\%$

A standard Z table is used to determine the area under the curve. The area under the curve represents probability.

Note: A standard Z table can be found in the Appendix of this book. This particular table provides probabilities on the left side. When using other tables, verify which probability it is providing. Tables may accumulate area under the curve from the left or right tail. Graphically depicting the problem statement and practical interpretation of the results is recommended.

Because the curve is symmetric, the area shown as yield would be $1 - P(z > 1) = 0.841$ or 84.1%.

In accordance with the equation, Z can be calculated for any "point of interest," x.

Variation

The following figure shows three normal distributions with the same mean. What differs between the distributions is the variation.

Three Normal Distributions

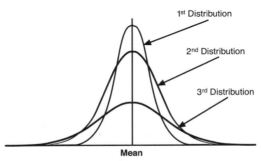

The first distribution displays less variation or dispersion about the mean. The second distribution displays more variation and would have a greater standard deviation. The third distribution displays even more variation.

Short-term vs. Long-term Variation

The duration over which data is collected will determine whether short-term or long-term variation has been captured within the subgroup.

There are two types of variation in every process: *common cause variation and special cause variation*. Common cause variation is completely random (i.e., the next data point's specific value cannot be predicted). It is the natural

---

variation of the process. Special cause variation is the nonrandom variation in the process. It is the result of an event, an action, or a series of events or actions. The nature and causes of special cause variation are different for every process.

Short-term data is data that is collected from the process in subgroups. Each subgroup is collected over a short length of time to capture common cause variation only (i.e., data is not collected across different shifts because variation can exist from operator to operator). Thus, the subgroup consists of "like" things collected over a narrow time frame and is considered a "snapshot in time" of the process. For example, a process may use several raw material lots per shift. A representative short-term sample may consist of CTQ measurements within one lot.

Long-term data is considered to contain both special and common causes of variation that are typically observed when all of the input variables have varied over their full range. To continue with the same example, long-term data would consist of several raw material lots measured across several short-term samples.

Process Variation Over Time

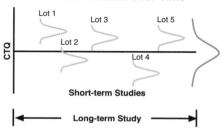

Processes tend to exhibit more variation in the long term than in the short term. Long-term variability is made up of short-term variability and process drift. The shift from short term to long term can be quantified by taking both short-term and long-term samples.

Long-term Drift

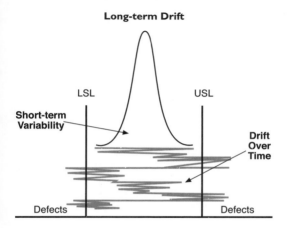

On average, short-term process means tend to shift and drift by 1.5 sigmas.

$$Z_{lt} = Z_{st} - 1.5$$

(The short-term Z (Z_{st}) is also known as the benchmark sigma value. The Rolled Throughput Yield (RTY) section of this book discusses several related Six Sigma metrics used to evaluate processes.)

A Six Sigma process would have six standard deviations between the mean and the closest specification limit for a short-term capability study. The following figure illustrates the Z-score relationship to the Six Sigma philosophy:

Z-Score Relationship
To Six Sigma Philosophy

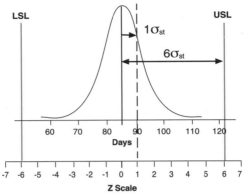

In a Six Sigma process, customer satisfaction and business objectives are robust to shifts caused by process or product variation.

Six Sigma as a Statistical Measure

DPMO is directly related to Z. A reference chart to convert from Z_{lt} to DPMO can be found in the Appendix of this book. This chart already includes the 1.5 sigma shift. For example, shifting a Six Sigma process 1.5 sigma creates 3.4 defects per million opportunities. Recall our previous example with a $Z_{st} = 1.0$. If so, then $Z_{lt} = 1.0 - 1.5 = -0.5$. From the conversion table, the long-term DPMO is 691,500 or 69.15% defects. The yield is (1 - 0.6915) = 0.3085 or 30.85%.

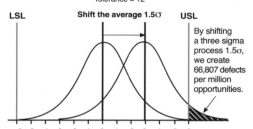

Three Sigma Process
Average = 0
St. Dev. = 2
Tolerance = 12

LSL

Shift the average 1.5σ

USL

By shifting
a three sigma
process 1.5σ,
we create
66,807 defects
per million
opportunities.

-6 -5 -4 -3 -2 -1 0 1 2 3 4 5 6

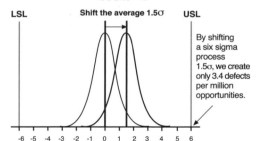

Six Sigma Process
Average = 0
St. Dev. = 1
Tolerance = 12

LSL

Shift the average 1.5σ

USL

By shifting
a six sigma
process
1.5σ, we create
only 3.4 defects
per million
opportunities.

-6 -5 -4 -3 -2 -1 0 1 2 3 4 5 6

Notes

MEASUREMENT SYSTEMS ANALYSIS

Why use it?

In practice, many measurement systems produce unreliable data. If the data are unreliable, decisions made on the basis of the data are questionable. If measurement is a significant source of variability, organizations can make bad decisions, such as reject good units and/or accept bad units. Therefore, it must be determined if the measurement system is reliable before the baseline capability can be determined.

A Measurement Systems Analysis (MSA) is used to determine if the measurement system is a significant source of variability and if so, what actions are necessary to repair or replace the measurement system. Doing so allows the organization to properly accept good units and properly reject bad units, thus establishing the true quality level. Note that many problems have been solved simply by fixing the measurement system.

What does it do?

A Measurement Systems Analysis (MSA) is a series of designed tests that allow an organization to determine whether its measurement system is reliable in terms of bias, linearity, stability, discrimination, and precision.

There are two types of MSAs. The choice of which one to use depends on whether the data are variable or attribute. In many systems, there are a few areas to consider in conducting an MSA:

- Measuring or making a determination
- Inputting the data
- Manipulating the data
- Reporting the data

Consider the likelihood of error in each of these areas and conduct the MSA where errors are most likely to occur. In many cases, the most likely sources of error involve the human element, especially measuring and inputting.

Variable Data

For variable data, the measurement system is comprised of the units being measured, the gauge, the operators, and their methods. The tree diagram below shows the relationship of the sources of variation.

Sources of Variation

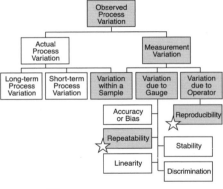

When conducting an MSA, the organization must evaluate the bias, linearity, stability, discrimination, and variability (or precision) in the measurement system.

The *bias* is the difference between the observed average value of measurements and a known standard or master value. If bias exists in the average measured value, the measurement system may require calibration.

The *linearity* determines whether a bias exists in the measurement system over its operating range. For example, thermometers or scales may have negative bias at the low end of the scale and positive bias at the high end of the scale.

The *stability* determines the measurement system's ability to measure consistently over time such that the measurement system does not drift.

The *discrimination* or resolution of the measurement system is the ability to detect small changes in the characteristic being measured.

Variability or Precision:

- The *repeatability* is the ability of the measurement system to return the same measured value when one operator takes repeated measurements of the same unit

- The *reproducibility* is the degree of agreement when multiple operators measure the same characteristic on the same unit

Attribute Data

For attribute data, the measurement system is comprised of the units being measured, the gauge, the operators, and their methods. In this MSA, the operators are frequently the gauge, and the evaluation consists of how well they judge a characteristic to either determine its acceptability (yes/no) or properly rate it on a scale. Examples include operators inspecting rolls of cloth for defects or an operator's ability to complete a purchase order form properly. This type of MSA can determine whether:

- An operator can repeat his or her measures when evaluating many units multiple times (*within operator* variation)

- An operator not only repeats his or her own measures on multiple units, but can match those measures to known standards for the units (accuracy)

- Multiple operators can match the measurements of one another on multiple units (*between operator* variation)

- Multiple operators not only match the measurements of one another on multiple units, but can all match the known standard for these units

How do I do it?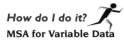

MSA for Variable Data

A. Bias - To determine whether bias exists in the system:

1. Obtain a known standard that represents a value within the normal range of the characteristic of interest

2. Have one operator with one gauge measure the known standard a minimum of ten times, record these values, and calculate the average

3. Compare the average to the known standard:
   - If the average is less than the known standard, then offset the gauge positively by this amount
   - If the average is greater than the known standard, then offset the gauge negatively by this amount

Example:

A known standard was obtained and certified to be 0.500". One operator using one gauge measured this standard

---

ten times and determined the average value to be 0.496".
Because the average value is 0.004" less than the standard, the gauge must be positively offset by 0.004".

Bias

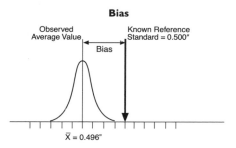

B. Linearity - To determine whether bias exists over the operating range of the gauge:

1. Identify four or more standard/reference units that span the likely range over which the measurement system is to be used

2. Identify one operator to determine the bias of the gauge over the operating range of the process variation

3. Have the operator measure each reference unit at least ten times and then calculate the bias for each of the units

4. Create a scatter plot with the standard/reference units on the x axis and the bias values on the y axis

5. Create a regression equation for this data and determine whether the goodness of fit term (R^2) is acceptable

The slope of the regression line determines the linearity. Generally, the lower the absolute value of the slope, the better the linearity; the converse is also true (the higher the absolute value of the slope, the worse the linearity).

Example:

A linearity study was conducted in which six samples that spanned the operating range of the gauge were identified and certified. (Certified is when a unit is measured with a known high precision instrument.) One operator measured each of the six samples ten times and the bias for the six units was calculated. The data was graphed using a fitted line plot and the fit was assessed using R^2.

Linearity

Regression Plot

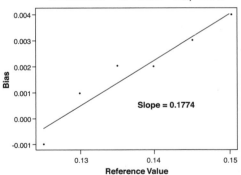

Bias = -0.0225238 + 0.177143 Reference Value
S = 0.0005255 R^2 = 92.6% R^2_{adj} = 90.7%

Slope = 0.1774

If the system is determined to be nonlinear, check for a defective gauge, wrong standard/reference values, incorrect operator methods of measuring, or an improperly calibrated gauge.

C. Stability - To determine whether the measurement system's bias is drifting over time:

1. Obtain a standard/reference unit that falls in the mid-range of the production values

2. On a regular basis (weekly or monthly), measure the standard/reference value three to five times

3. Plot this data in an Xbar-R control chart

4. Monitor these charts regularly to determine whether the gauge needs to be calibrated

5. If desired, create the same control charts for reference values on the low and high side of production

Example:

A standard/reference value is measured three times on a weekly basis. The data is plotted in an Xbar-R control chart (which combines two charts of the same data, an Xbar chart and an R chart).

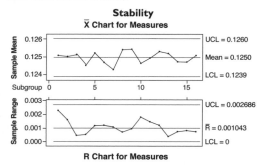

Stability
$\bar{X}$ Chart for Measures

R Chart for Measures

Both charts are used to determine the stability or repeatability of the measurements over time. The R chart captures the **within subgroup** (multiple readings of the same part) variation over time. The R chart generates the control limits for the Xbar chart. The Xbar chart of the week-to-week averages captures the **between subgroup** variation. Because the Xbar-R chart is in control, the measurement system is exhibiting good stability over time. If there were an issue with stability, a design of experiments could be applied to determine the contributors to the poor stability.

Discrimination

Discrimination is the ability of the measurement system to detect small changes in the characteristic of interest. As a general rule, the measurement system should be able to discriminate to one-tenth the tolerance range (USL - LSL).

Example:

If a critical characteristic of a part is its length, and the lower and upper specification limits are 1.500" and 1.550" respectively, the measurement system should be able to measure to one-tenth the tolerance or (1.550" - 1.500")/10 = 0.005". Therefore, at a minimum, any gauge used needs to measure to 0.005".

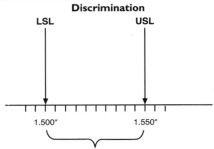

Discrimination

LSL   USL

1.500"   1.550"

The measurement system must be able to resolve
the tolerance to ten equal divisions of 0.005".

Consider instead in this example, if the measurement system could only measure to 0.050". In this case, these parts could only be classified as meeting the upper or lower specification limit and nothing in between. Therefore, this gauge would not provide adequate discrimination to properly accept or reject parts.

MSA Components of Variation

Any measurement of a part not only measures the true part value, but also measures any variability that may exist because of the poor repeatability of the gauge and/or the poor reproducibility of the operators and their methods of measuring. Obviously, it is desirable to ascertain the true part value free of any other source of variability to determine the true capability of the process. A test known as a Gauge Repeatability & Reproducibility (GR&R) test is conducted to determine whether excessive variability exists in the measurement system. This test is designed such that the product variability and the measurement system variability (also known as measurement system error or precision, P) can be partitioned from the total variability as shown in the following figure:

MSA Components of Variation

$$\hat{\sigma}^2\ Total\ =\ \hat{\sigma}^2\ product\ +\ \hat{\sigma}^2\ ms$$

Total variability = product variability + measurement system variability

$$\hat{\sigma}^2\ repeatability\ +\ \hat{\sigma}^2\ reproducibility$$

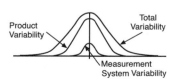

Product Variability

Total Variability

Measurement System Variability

As shown in the figure, measurement system variability can further be partitioned into:

- Measurement system repeatability: The ability of one operator using one gauge to measure one part multiple times with minimal variability

- Measurement system reproducibility: The ability of multiple operators to produce similar average measures for multiple parts, with minimal variability in the average measured values

Once all of these variances have been calculated, the organization can determine whether the measurement system is reliable based on the following calculations. If the measurement system is deemed unreliable, these variances can help determine whether the problem is repeatability and/or reproducibility.

Gauge R&R Acceptance Criteria

- *Percent Tolerance* is the variability of the measurement system compared to the tolerance range ($6\sigma_{ms}$ / (USL–LSL)). If this value is less than 10%, the gauge is excellent. If it is 10%–30%, the gauge is marginal. If it is greater than 30%, the gauge is unacceptable.

- *Percent Process* is the variability of the measurement system compared to the historical process variability ($6\sigma_{ms}$ / $6\sigma_{historical}$). If this value is less than 10%, the gauge is excellent. If it is 10%–30%, the gauge is marginal. If it is greater than 30%, the gauge is unacceptable.

How do I do a Continuous GR&R test?

1. Identify the characteristic on the unit to be measured, the gauge, and the operators who use the gauge

2. Identify a number of units (typically ten units) that span the range of the long-term process variability

   - This may require samples to be collected over several days or weeks

3. Conduct the GR&R in the environment where the measurement normally takes place

4. Estimate repeatability and reproducibility by conducting a test using three operators and ten units. The units need to be measured at least twice by each operator

   - This test should be randomized; therefore, have the first operator measure the ten units in random order, then have the second operator measure the ten units in random order, and then the third operator. After the operators have measured all of the units once, they are to measure the units again in random order to obtain the repeat measures. There should be a total of sixty measures in this designed test (3 x 10 x 2)

5. Calculate the variances using the ANOVA method

   - Many software packages can be used to calculate variances using the ANOVA method

6. Interpret the results graphically and analytically to determine whether the measurement system is acceptable, needs repair, or must be replaced

---

Example:

A DMAIC team needed to determine the baseline capability of the diameter of a wire. However, prior to determining capability, the team knew they had to conduct an MSA. In this example, the tolerance range (USL–LSL) is .07 mm, and the historical standard deviation is 0.015 mm. The team selected ten wires, the gauge used to measure these wires, and three operators to use this gauge. They then created the following sampling plan:

MSA Sampling Plan

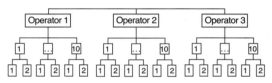

- Three operators, ten parts, two trial measures
- Each operator measures the same ten parts, twice in random order.

The following figure shows what the graphical output of this MSA would look like.

Gauge R&R (ANOVA) Report for Measurements

Gage name:
Date of study:

Reported by:
Tolerance:
Misc:

MSA Graphical Results

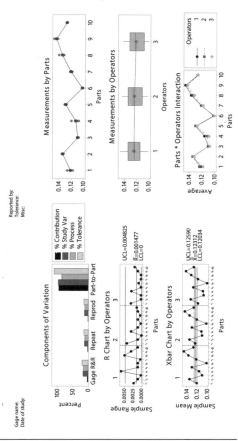

Interpreting the graphical results:

When interpreting the results, it is important to always assess the range chart (R chart) for stability first. Assessing the range chart for stability ensures that there are no special causes. (Special causes should be corrected and the MSA repeated.) Special causes in the range chart will increase the average range and in turn will inflate the distance between the control limits in the average chart. Secondly, it is important to assess discrimination from the range chart. A recommended guideline is to ensure that at least five levels of possible values in the range chart, including zero, are evident. A lack of discrimination may also be the result of rounding-off values.

Captured in the range chart are measures within part. This variation is reflected between the control limits on the average Xbar Chart by Operators. Captured in the average chart is the part-to-part variation between operators. In our example, most of the averages are outside of the control limits on the average chart, indicating that the variation *within subgroup* (measurement within part) is less than the variation *between subgroup* (part-to-part). Ideally, we want to be able to detect part-to-part variation, so out-of-control points on the average chart are desired in this case. Measurement variation should be much less than part-to-part variation, as indicated in this example.

Software packages offer charts other than just the Xbar and R charts. The components of variation bar chart in this Minitab® software output indicates that the largest source of variation is part-to-part. Repeatability and reproducibility are comparable.

Reproducibility is evidenced in the average chart between operators 1, 2, and 3. The "Measurements by Operators" chart is a boxplot of all the measurements for each operator. Because the operators measured the same parts, the same results in terms of boxplot shape and average value would be expected between operators.

Because the sampling plan is "crossed" (see the Multi-Vari Charts chapter in this book for more information on crossed designs) between operator and part, there is a potential for an operator-by-part interaction. This is indicated by the crossing lines in the "Parts*Operators Interaction" chart, which shows that not all operators measure the same parts the same way.

Interpreting the analytical results:

The following figure shows the MSA analytical results for the wire example previously cited.

MSA Analytical Results

```
Process tolerance = 0.07
Historical standard deviation = 0.015


                                   Study Var   %Tolerance    %Process
Source              StdDev (SD)    (6 × SD)    (SV/Toler)    (SV/Proc)
Total Gage R&R      0.0023185      0.0139111   19.87         15.46
  Repeatability     0.0016583      0.0099499   14.21         11.06
  Reproducibility   0.0016203      0.0097220   13.89         10.80
    Operators       0.0016203      0.0097220   13.89         10.80
Part-To-Part        0.0130220      0.0781319   111.62        86.81
Total Variation     0.0132268      0.0793606   113.37        88.18
```

According to these results, the measurement system is marginal because both Percent Tolerance and Percent Process are between 10% and 30%. (See the GR&R Acceptance Criteria section earlier in this chapter.)

The graphs indicate that the operators may be having trouble measuring sample #4 and that operator #3 is measuring consistently lower values than the other two operators. The team may decide to address these two issues, fix them, and run another GR&R before proceeding.

Destructive Testing

In many instances, the characteristic being measured (e.g., strength or moisture) is destroyed during the measurement, so a second or third operator cannot measure the same part.

Typically, a GR&R uses ten parts, three operators, and two measures per part for a total of 60 measures. To conduct the GR&R where the parts are destroyed, ten batches with six parts per batch are needed, for a total of 60 parts that are measured. The batches must be produced such that they represent the long-term variability of the process and the parts contained within a batch are assumed to be consistent.

Each operator will measure two parts per batch and the results will be analyzed. This destructive GR&R uses a nested ANOVA to analyze the data vs. a crossed ANOVA in the nondestructive test. (Nested refers to parts being unique to the operator.)

MSA for Attribute Data

When the characteristic to be measured is attribute in nature (e.g., the correct name in a field on a form, the correct color blue, or a rank on a scale by an operator), then the organization would need to conduct an Attribute Agreement Analysis. Depending on the test, the objective of the study would be to ensure operators can either discern between good and bad or rank a characteristic on a scale and get the correct answer. In this test, the operator is frequently the gauge.

How do I do an Attribute Agreement Analysis?

1. Identify 30 to 100 items to be evaluated

   • Typically more samples are needed in an attribute study because of the nature of data

---

2. Have a person who has knowledge of the customer requirements for this characteristic rate these items on the scale that is used in daily operations

   - Record the person's responses for all 30 to 100 items in a column of data called "attribute" or "reference standard"

3. Identify the people who need to measure the items

4. Have the first person rate all 30 to 100 items in random order and record these values

   - Repeat this step for each subsequent person recording this data

5. Repeat step four such that each operator has a chance at a repeat measure and record this data

Several important measures from this test are identified in the following example.

Example Attribute Agreement Analysis Measures

Known Population		Operator #1		Operator #2		Operator #3	
Sample	Attribute	Try #1	Try #2	Try #1	Try #2	Try #1	Try #2
1	pass	pass	pass	pass	pass	fail	fail
2	pass	pass	pass	pass	pass	fail	fail
3	fail	fail	fail	fail	pass	fail	fail
4	fail	fail	fail	fail	fail	fail	fail
5	fail	fail	fail	pass	fail	fail	fail
6	pass	pass	pass	pass	pass	pass	pass

1. Within Appraisers (similar to repeatability). The number of times an operator can repeat the measured value. If an operator measured 30 items twice and successfully repeated the measures 26 times, then he or she had an 86.6% success rate.

Each operator will have a success rate for their repeat measures

2. **Each Appraiser vs. Standard** (similar to accuracy). The number of times an operator not only repeats the measures, but these repeats match the known standard. Although an operator may have successfully repeated their measures 86.6% of the time, the measure may have only matched the known standard 23 times out of 30, for a 76.6% success rate. This implies that an operator may not understand the criteria for the known standard

3. **Between Appraisers** (similar to reproducibility). The number of times all of the operators match their repeat measures. If three operators evaluate 30 parts and all of the operators match their repeats 22 times, then this is a 73.3% success rate

4. **All Appraisers vs. Standard** (similar to total gauge R&R). The number of times all of the operators match their repeat measures and all these measures match the known standards. If three operators match all of these measures 20 times out of 30, then this is a success rate of 66.6%. With ordinal data, a better measure is Kendall's coefficient because it takes into account the magnitude of the errors (e.g., if the standard rating is 3, an appraised value of 4 is better than an appraised value of 5). Kendall's values range from 0 to 1

This All Appraisers vs. Standard measure is the measure used to determine the effectiveness of the measurement system. In general, it should be greater than 80% (preferably 90%), assuming that the study was done with three operators and two trials. Generally, Kendall's coefficients of 0.9 or greater are considered very good. If the value is less than 80%, then opportunities for improvement need to be identified. Typically, the solution is either training all of the operators, a better definition of the known standard, or an improvement to the environment in the area where the item is being measured.

Example:

When a customer places an order, a system operator is responsible for finding information in a database and then transferring that information to the order form. Recently, customers have been receiving the wrong product, and the data suggest that the problem may be in transferring this information. For the team to determine the capability of this process, an Attribute Agreement Analysis must first be conducted. To do this, the team creates 30 different fake orders, with known correct answers. Next the operators are asked to find the required information in the database to determine whether the operators can get the correct answer or not. The answers to this test are input into Minitab® and an Attribute Agreement Analysis is conducted.

Attribute Agreement Analysis Effectiveness

```
All Appraisers vs Standard

Assessment Agreement

# Inspected  # Matched  Percent      95% CI
       30           23    76.67  (57.72, 90.07)

# Matched: All appraisers' assessments agree with the known standard.
```

According to these results, the measurement system is unacceptable because the All Appraisers vs. Standard assessment agreement is less than 80%.

Notes

ROLLED THROUGHPUT YIELD

Why use it?

Rolled Throughput Yield (RTY) is used to assess the true yield of a process that includes waste (a hidden factory). A hidden factory adds no value to the customer and involves fixing things that weren't done right the first time.

What does it do?

RTY determines the probability of a product or service making it through a multistep process without being scrapped or ever reworked.

How do I do it?

There are two methods to measure RTY:

Method 1 assesses defects per unit (dpu), when all that is known is the final number of units produced and the number of defects:

- A *defect* is defined as something that does not conform to a known and accepted customer standard

- A *unit* is the product, information, or service used or purchased by a customer

- An *opportunity for a defect* is a measured characteristic on a unit that needs to conform to a customer standard (e.g., the ohms of an electrical resistor, the diameter of a pen, the time it takes to deliver a package, or the address field on a form)

- The term *defective* is used when the entire unit is deemed unacceptable because of the nonconformance of any one of the opportunities for a defect

Shown in the following diagram are six units, each containing five opportunities for a defect.

Opportunities for a Defect

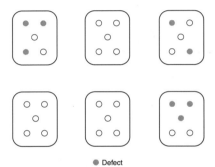

● Defect

Given that any one defect can cause a unit to be defective, it appears the yield of this process is 50%. This, however, is a small sample and may not tell the whole story. Assuming that defects are randomly distributed, the special form of the Poisson distribution formula

$$RTY = e^{-dpu}$$

can be used to estimate the number of units with zero defects (i.e., the RTY).

The previous figure showed eight defects over six units, resulting in 1.33 dpu. Entering this into our formula:

$$RTY = e^{-1.33}$$
$$RTY = 0.264$$

According to this calculation, for a much larger sample with a random distribution of defects, this process can expect an average of 26.4% defect-free units that have not been reworked (which is much different than the assumed 50%).

Method 2 determines throughput yield (Y_{tp}), when the specific yields at each opportunity for a defect are known.

If, on a unit, the yield at each opportunity for a defect is known (i.e., the five yields at each opportunity in the previous figure), then these yields can be multiplied together to determine the RTY. The yields at each opportunity for a defect are known as the throughput yields, which can be calculated as

$$Y_{tp} = e^{-dpu}$$

for that specific opportunity for a defect for attribute data, and

$$Y_{tp} = 1 - P(\text{defect})$$

for variable data, where P(defect) is the probability of a defect based on the normal distribution.

Shown in the following figure is one unit from the previous figure in which the associated Y_{tp}'s at each opportunity were measured for many units.

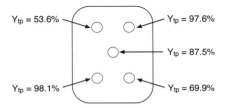

**Throughput Yield
at Each Opportunity for a Defect**

Y_{tp} = 53.6%

Y_{tp} = 97.6%

Y_{tp} = 87.5%

Y_{tp} = 98.1%

Y_{tp} = 69.9%

Multiplying these yields together results in the RTY:

$$RTY = Y_{tp1} \times Y_{tp2} \times Y_{tp3} \times Y_{tp4} \times Y_{tp5}$$

$$RTY = 0.536 \times 0.976 \times 0.875 \times 0.981 \times 0.699$$

$$RTY = 0.314$$

According to this calculation, an average of 31.4% defect-free units that have not been reworked can be expected.

Defects Per Million Opportunities

Why use it?

Defects per million opportunities (DPMO) helps to determine the capability of a process.

What does it do?

DPMO allows for the calculation of capability at one or more opportunities and ultimately, if desired, for the entire organization.

How do I do it?

Calculating DPMO depends on whether the data is variable or attribute and if there is one or more than one opportunity for a defect.

If there is:

- *One opportunity with variable data*, use the Z transform to determine the probability of observing a defect, then multiply by 1 million
- *One opportunity with attribute data*, calculate the proportion of defects, then multiply by 1 million
- *More than one opportunity with both variable and/or attribute data*, use one of two methods below to determine DPMO

1. **Calculate the total Defects Per Million Opportunities (DPMO)**

   - To calculate DPMO, sum the defects and sum the total opportunities for a defect, then divide the defects by the total opportunities and multiply by 1 million

   Example:

   If there are eight defects and thirty total opportunities for a defect, then

   $$DPMO = (8/30) \times 1,000,000 = 266,667$$

   - When using this method to evaluate multiple opportunity variable data, convert the calculated DPMO into defects and opportunities for each variable, then sum them to get total defects and opportunities

   Example:

   If one step in a process has a DPMO of 50,000 and another step has a DPMO of 100,000, there are 150,000 total defects for 2 million opportunities or 75,000 DPMO overall.

2. **Calculate the average yield per opportunity, also known as the normalized yield (Y_{na})**

- To calculate Y_{na} from RTY, assuming there are m opportunities per unit, take RTY to the 1/m power

$$Y_{na} = RTY^{(1/m)}$$

To calculate RTY from Y_{na}, take Y_{na} to the mth power

$$RTY = Y_{na}{}^m$$

$$DPMO = (1-Y_{na}) \times 1{,}000{,}000$$

Example:

If there are five opportunities per unit and the RTY is 0.264, then:

$$Y_{na} = 0.264^{(1/5)}$$

$$Y_{na} = 0.766$$

$$DPMO = (1-0.766) \times 1{,}000{,}000 = 234{,}000$$

The difference between DPMO and Y_{na} is that Y_{na} is an estimate based on the Poisson distribution, and DPMO is an actual calculation. As the defect rate falls below 10%, these values converge.

# SIGMA VALUES

Why use it?

Sigma values are calculated to determine a baseline performance for an opportunity, process, or product. Sigma values can also be used to fairly compare different products, services, information, or divisions within an organization and, if desired, benchmark the like.

Note: Sigma has many different definitions and can be used in many different ways:

- As a benchmark
- As a population's standard deviation
- As a baseline measure that describes how far a process mean is from the nearest specification
- As a measure of distance (e.g., two process means are 4.5 sigma apart)

What does it do?

Sigma helps establish baselines and set targets, goals, and objectives against which progress can be measured.

How do I do it?

Once DPMO has been calculated, sigma values can be looked up in a table. Tables may be found in many common computer software packages and in appendices of statistical books. Remember that it is necessary to understand whether the data collected is short term or long term, as it may be necessary to either add or subtract 1.5 to the lookup value.

Partial DPMO to Z Table

DPMO	Z	DPMO	Z	DPMO	Z	DPMO	Z	DPMO	Z
500000	0.000	95000	1.311	2500	2.807	480	3.302	75	3.791
480000	0.050	90000	1.341	2400	2.820	460	3.314	70	3.808
460000	0.100	85000	1.372	2300	2.834	440	3.326	65	3.826
440000	0.151	80000	1.405	2200	2.848	420	3.339	60	3.846
420000	0.202	75000	1.440	2100	2.863	400	3.353	55	3.867
400000	0.253	70000	1.476	2000	2.878	380	3.367	50	3.891
380000	0.305	65000	1.514	1900	2.894	360	3.382	45	3.916
360000	0.358	60000	1.555	1800	2.911	340	3.398	40	3.944
340000	0.412	55000	1.598	1700	2.929	320	3.414	35	3.976
320000	0.468	50000	1.645	1600	2.948	300	3.432	30	4.013
300000	0.524	45000	1.695	1500	2.968	280	3.450	25	4.056
280000	0.583	40000	1.751	1400	2.989	260	3.470	20	4.107
260000	0.643	35000	1.812	1300	3.011	240	3.492	15	4.173
240000	0.706	30000	1.881	1200	3.036	220	3.515	10	4.265
220000	0.772	25000	1.960	1100	3.062	200	3.540	5	4.417
200000	0.842	20000	2.054	1000	3.090	180	3.568	4	4.465
180000	0.915	15000	2.170	900	3.121	160	3.599	3	4.526
160000	0.994	10000	2.326	800	3.156	140	3.633	2	4.611
140000	1.080	5000	2.576	700	3.195	120	3.673	1	4.753
120000	1.175	4000	2.652	600	3.239	100	3.719	0.5	4.892
100000	1.282	3000	2.748	500	3.291	80	3.775	0.1	5.199

Not Shifted: Long-term DPMO will give long-term Z.

Short-term data is assumed to be free of special causes. For example, data collected over one shift does not allow any special causes due to differences in shift. In a transactional process, short-term data could measure the performance of one administrator over one day.

Long-term data is considered to contain both special and random (common cause) variation, typically observed when the input variables have varied over their full range.

Processes tend to exhibit more variation in the long term than the short term. Shown below is a process in which subgroups of data were collected on a daily basis (small bell curves) for an extended period of time. The shifting and drifting of the subgroup averages (the shift factor) is due to many special causes, such as tool wear, different operators working the process, different lots of raw materials, etc. It has been demonstrated that because of these special causes, the subgroup means tend to shift and drift, on average, 1.5 standard deviations.

Subgroup Drift

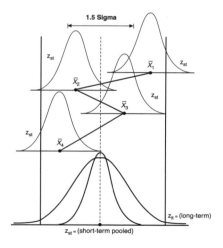

How do I practically use the shift factor?

If short-term data has been collected, then the calculation will be to baseline a process to determine a short-term sigma (Z_{st}). If long-term data is not available but long-term performance needs to be estimated, then 1.5 can be subtracted from the Z_{st} to estimate long-term performance. (The opposite also is true: to estimate short-term performance, add 1.5 to the Z_{lt}.)

Using the Shift Factor

		To know:	
		Z_{st}	Z_{lt}
		Short-term capability	Long-term capability
Z_{st}	Short-term data	✔	**Subtract 1.5**
Z_{lt}	Long-term data	**Add 1.5**	✔

$$Z_{lt} = Z_{st} - 1.5$$

Note: Use 1.5 as the shift factor until enough data on the process has been collected to distinguish between long-term and short-term variation. Once enough data has been collected, the exact shift factor for the process can then be determined, although it is difficult and data intensive to do so when using attribute data.

Example:

A DPMO of 266,667 was calculated in the previous chapter. If we consider it to be long-term data, looking up the sigma value in a table shows a long-term sigma value of 0.62. If we need to report a short-term sigma value, we can add 1.5 to the sigma value to obtain a short-term sigma value of 2.12.

PROCESS CAPABILITY

Why use it?

Process capability refers to the capability of a process to consistently make a product that meets a customer-specified specification range (tolerance). Capability indices are used to predict the performance of a process by comparing the width of process variation to the width of the specified tolerance. They are used extensively in many industries and only have meaning if the process being studied is stable (in statistical control).

What does it do?

Capability indices allow calculations for both short-term (C_p and C_{pk}) and/or long-term (P_p and P_{pk}) performance for a process whose output is measured using variable data at a specific opportunity for a defect. Note that capability indices should be calculated only after the DMAIC team has demonstrated that the measurement system is acceptable and the process is stable.

Short-Term Capability Indices

The short-term capability indices C_p and C_{pk} are measures calculated using the short-term process standard deviation. Because the short-term process variation is used, these measures are free of subgroup drift in the data and take into account only the *within subgroup* variation.

C_p is a ratio of the customer-specified tolerance to six standard deviations of the short-term process variation. C_p is calculated without regard to location of the data mean within the tolerance, so it gives an indication of what the process could achieve if the mean of the data were centered between the specification limits. Because of this assumption, C_p is sometimes referred to as the process potential.

C_{pk} is a ratio of the distance between the process average (Xbar) and the closest specification limit, to three standard deviations of the short-term process variation. Because C_{pk} takes into account location of the data mean within the tolerance, it is a more realistic measure of the process capability. C_{pk} is sometimes referred to as the process performance.

Long-Term Capability Indices

The long-term capability indices P_p and P_{pk} are measures calculated using the long-term process standard deviation. Because the long-term process variation is used, these measures take into account subgroup drift in the data as well as the *within subgroup* variation.

P_p is a ratio of the customer-specified tolerance to six standard deviations of the long-term process variation. Like C_p, P_p is calculated without regard to location of the data mean within the tolerance.

P_{pk} is a ratio of the distance between the process average and the closest specification limit, to three standard deviations of the long-term process variation. Like C_{pk}, P_{pk} takes into account the location of the data mean within the tolerance. Because P_{pk} uses the long-term variation in the process and takes into account the process centering within the specified tolerance, it is a good indicator of the process performance the customer is seeing.

What is a good C_p/C_{pk} or P_p/P_{pk} value?

Because both C_p and C_{pk} are ratios of the tolerance width to the process variation, larger values of C_p and C_{pk} are better. The larger the C_p and C_{pk}, the wider the tolerance width relative to the process variation. The same is also true for P_p and P_{pk}.

What determines a "good" value depends on the definition of "good." A C_p of 1.33 is approximately equivalent to a short-term Z of 4. A P_{pk} of 1.33 is approximately equivalent to a long-term Z of 4. However, a Six Sigma process typically has a short-term Z of 6 or a long-term Z of 4.5.

Cpk	Zst	Ppk	Zlt	DPMOlt	%lt	Interpretation
2	6	1.5	4.5	3.4	0.00034%	World Class
1.5	4.5	1	3	1700	0.17%	Typical
1	3	0.5	1.5	67000	6.70%	Sub Par

How do I do it?

1. Ensure that the operational definition is correct, the MSA is acceptable, and the process is stable

2. Determine the data type (continuous vs. attribute)

3. Determine the nature of the data (short- vs. long-term)

4. Collect data from the process (Try to collect at least 25 subgroups)

5. Calculate capability

The type of data available (short-term or long-term) will determine whether C_p/C_{pk} or P_p/P_{pk} can be calculated. The following mathematical formulas are used to calculate these indices.

$$C_p = (USL - LSL)/6\sigma_{st}$$
Where σ_{st} = short-term pooled standard deviation

$$C_{pk} = \min (C_{pl}, C_{pu})$$
Where $C_{pl} = (Xbar-LSL)/3\sigma_{st}$ and $C_{pu} = (USL-Xbar)/3\sigma_{st}$

$$P_p = (USL - LSL)/6\sigma_{lt}$$
Where σ_{lt} = long-term standard deviation

$$P_{pk} = \min (P_{pl}, P_{pu})$$
Where $P_{pl} = (Xbar-LSL)/3\sigma_{lt}$ and $P_{pu} = (USL-Xbar)/3\sigma_{lt}$

Capability Indices

Short-term Capability Indices

$$C_p = \frac{USL - LSL}{6\,\sigma_{st}}$$

$$C_{pk} = \min\,(C_{pk(USL)}, C_{pk\,(LSL)})$$

$$C_{pk(USL)} = \frac{(USL - \bar{X})}{3\,\sigma_{st}}$$

$$C_{pk(LSL)} = \frac{(\bar{X} - LSL)}{3\,\sigma_{st}}$$

Long-term Capability Indices

$$P_p = \frac{USL - LSL}{6\,\sigma_{lt}}$$

$$P_{pk} = \min\,(P_{pk(USL)}, P_{pk\,(LSL)})$$

$$P_{pk(USL)} = \frac{(USL - \bar{X})}{3\,\sigma_{lt}}$$

$$P_{pk(LSL)} = \frac{(\bar{X} - LSL)}{3\,\sigma_{lt}}$$

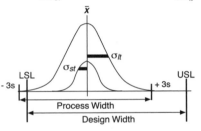

Example in Manufacturing:

Suppose the diameter of a spark plug is a critical dimension that needs to conform to lower and upper customer specification limits of 0.480" and 0.490", respectively. Five randomly selected spark plugs are measured in every work shift. Each sample of five measurements is called a subgroup. Subgroups have been collected for three months on a stable process. The average of all the data was 0.487". The short-term standard deviation has been calculated and was determined to be 0.0013". The long-term standard deviation was determined to be 0.019".

To calculate C_p and C_{pk}:

$$C_p = (0.490" - 0.480") / (6 \times 0.0013) = 0.010/0.0078 = 1.28$$

$$C_{pl} = (0.487 - 0.480) / (3 \times 0.0013) = 0.007/0.0039 = 1.79$$

$$C_{pu} = (0.490 - 0.487) / (3 \times 0.0013) = 0.003/0.0039 = 0.77$$

$$C_{pk} = \min (C_{pl}, C_{pu})$$

$$C_{pk} = \min (1.79, 0.77) = 0.77$$

To Calculate P_p and P_{pk}:

$$P_p = (0.490" - 0.480") / (6 \times 0.019) = 0.0100/0.114 = 0.09$$

$$P_{pl} = (0.487 - 0.480) / (3 \times 0.019) = 0.007/0.057 = 0.12$$

$$P_{pu} = (0.490 - 0.487) / (3 \times 0.019) = 0.003/0.057 = 0.05$$

$$P_{pk} = \min (P_{pl}, P_{pu})$$

$$P_{pk} = \min (0.12, 0.05) = 0.05$$

In this example, C_p is 1.28. Because C_p is the ratio of the specified tolerance to the process variation, a C_p value of 1.28 indicates that the process is potentially capable of delivering product that meets the specified tolerance (if the process is centered) about 99.9% of the time. Any improvements to the process to increase our value of 1.28 would require a reduction in the variability within our subgroups. C_p, however, is calculated without regard to the process centering within the specified tolerance. A centered process is rarely the case so a C_{pk} value must be calculated.

C_{pk} considers the location of the process data average. In this calculation, we are comparing the average of our process to the closest specification limit and dividing by three short-term standard deviations. In our example, C_{pk} is 0.77. In contrast to the C_p measurement, the C_{pk} measurement clearly shows that the process is incapable of consistently producing product that meets the specified tolerance. Any improvements to our process to increase our value of 0.77 would require a mean shift in the data towards the center of the tolerance range and/or a reduction in the *within subgroup* variation. (Note: For centered processes, C_p and C_{pk} will be the same.)

Our P_p is 0.09. Because P_p is the ratio of the specified tolerance to the process variation, a P_p value of 0.09 indicates that the process is incapable of consistently delivering product that meets the specified tolerance. Any improvements to the process to increase our value of 0.09 would require a reduction in the variability within and/or between subgroups. P_p, however, is calculated without regard to the process centering within the specified tolerance. A centered process is rarely the case, so a P_{pk} value, which accounts for lack of process centering, will surely indicate poor capability for our process as well. (Note: For both P_p and C_p, we assume no drifting of the subgroup averages.)

P_{pk} represents the actual long-term performance of the process and is the index that most likely represents what customers receive. In the example, P_{pk} is 0.05, confirming our P_p result of poor process performance. Any improvements to the process to increase our value of 0.05 would require a mean shift in the data towards the center of the tolerance and/or a reduction in the *within subgroup* and *between subgroup* variations.

Example in a Business Process:

Suppose a call center reports to its customers that it will resolve their issue within 15 minutes. This 15 minute time limit is the upper specification limit. It is desirable to resolve the issue as soon as possible; therefore, there is no lower specification limit. The call center operates 24 hours a day in eight-hour shifts. Six calls are randomly measured every shift and recorded for two months. An SPC chart shows the process is stable. The average of the data is 11.7 minutes, the short-term pooled standard deviation is 1.2 minutes, and the long-term standard deviation is 2.8 minutes.

To Calculate C_p and C_{pk}:

$$C_p = \text{cannot be calculated as there is no LSL}$$

$$C_{pl} = \text{undefined}$$

$$C_{pu} = (15 - 11.7)/(3 \times 1.2) = 3.3/3.6 = 0.92$$

$$C_{pk} = \min (C_{pl}, C_{pu}) = 0.92$$

To Calculate P_p and P_{pk}:

$$P_p = \text{cannot be calculated as there is no LSL}$$

$$P_{pl} = \text{undefined}$$

$$P_{pu} = (15 - 11.7)/(3 \times 2.8) = 3.3/8.4 = 0.39$$

$$P_{pk} = \min (P_{pl}, P_{pu}) = 0.39$$

In this example, we can only evaluate C_{pk} and P_{pk} as there is no lower limit. These numbers indicate that if we can eliminate *between subgroup* variation, we could achieve a process capability (P_{pk}) of 0.92, which is our current C_{pk}.

Notes

RISK ASSESSMENT AND MANAGEMENT

Why use it?

Assessing and managing risk helps to reduce risk and improve the chances of success of DMAIC projects. A risk management plan helps ensure that stakeholders understand the project risks. It provides a comprehensive approach to identify, analyze, and respond to risks before they happen.

What does it do?

Risks are uncertain events that may have a positive or negative effect on meeting program objectives. Risk management is an ongoing task to understand and reduce negative risk throughout a project. A risk management plan is a one-page document that identifies, analyzes, and provides a plan for responding to risk.

How do I do it?

1. Identify risks, consequences, and risk categories (scope, resource, and schedule)

2. Analyze risks in terms of probability (P) and impact (I)

   - Prioritize risks based on risk priority number (RPN = P x I)

3. Create a risk response plan with appropriate strategies

   - Use strategies, such as avoid, transfer, and mitigate strategies for high risk

- Use strategies, such as contingency and acceptance strategies for low risk

4. **Re-confirm the project charter, deploy the plan, monitor risks over time, and update the plan for each DMAIC phase review**

To identify risks, consider using brainstorming, checklists, examining assumptions, and historical information of risks that have occurred in similar projects. Each identified risk is assigned to one of three risk categories:

- Scope risks entail issues, such as scope creep and technical problems (for example: sponsor requests an expanded scope)

- Resource risks entail people, budget, and equipment constraints (for example: a key team member gets sick)

- Schedule risks entail planning errors and delays (for example: a decision is postponed until the next meeting)

Analyzing risks consists of two considerations:

- The probability (P) that an identified risk will occur (on a scale of 1-10)

- The impact (I) if the risk does occur (1-10)

These two considerations then drive risk priorities: RPN = P x I. The risk priorities then drive strategies within the risk response plan. Risks with high probability and high impact should have active plans to address them. Risks with low probability and low impact may be put on the watch list. The output is a list of prioritized risks.

There are a number of response strategies that can be considered for the prioritized risks:

- Avoiding a risk involves changing the project plan such that the risk is eliminated
- Transferring a risk involves shifting responsibility for responding to the risk
- Mitigating a risk involves reducing risk probability, risk impact, or both
- Contingency plans are executed only if a trigger event occurs
- Accepting a risk is appropriate when both probability and impact are low

Here are some tips for responding to risks in the three risk categories:

- Scope risks
  - Use explicit 'Is' and 'Is not' lists in the project charter
  - Use multi-generation plans to introduce changes in phases
  - Shield your project from scope creep
  - Use only well-established technology
- Resource risks
  - Ensure strong sponsorship
  - Co-locate the team if at all possible
  - Cross-train team members
- Schedule risks
  - Use historical data as an input for planning
  - Use worst-case analysis
  - Divide big projects into smaller projects

Example Risk Management Plan

Project name: Reduce lead time to repair equipment

Created: 02-08

Updated: 02-12

		H = 10	H = 10
		M = 5	M = 5
		L = 1	L = 1

ID	Risk statement	Consequence	Category	P	I	RPN	Type of response	Response plan	Owner	Status	P2	I2	RPN2
1	The key team member who knows how to collect the data may get sick	Team could not collect data, delaying the project until the key team member gets well	Resource	5	10	50	Mitigation	Cross-train 2 other team members to collect data	Sarah	Started to cross-train 02-10	5	5	25
2	Sponsor may ask us to address more types of equipment	It would take longer to complete the project	Scope	5	10	50	Mitigation	Specify what equipment is included and what is excluded in the charter	Sarah	Revised the charter and got approval 02-09	1	10	10
3													
4													
5													
6													
7													
8													

# ANALYZE PHASE

The purpose of the Analyze phase is to analyze information about the process and prove the root causes of the problem documented in the Measure phase. The major deliverables include:

- A list of the potential root causes
- Graphical analysis of stratified data
- Statistical analysis of the data
- A list of the proven root causes with an assessment of their effects

When the Analyze phase is complete, the team has enough understanding of the root causes to start identifying solutions in the Improve phase.

In the Analyze phase, the major tasks are to:

- Identify potential root causes
- Stratify and plot process data
- Confirm actual root causes with data and statistics
- Assess the effect of each confirmed root cause

ANALYZE

Step	Tools	Outputs
Identify potential root causes	Process Mapping, Cause & Effect Diagram, Cause & Effect Matrix, IS-IS NOT analysis	List of potential root causes
Stratify and plot process data	Graphical Analysis	Graphs of sources of variation
Confirm root causes with data and statistics	Hypothesis Testing, Regression Analysis	List of confirmed root causes
Assess effect of each confirmed root cause	Correlation	List of quantified effects, y = f(x) relationships

The chapters in this section include Cause and Effect Diagram, Graphical Analysis, Multi-Vari Charts, Central Limit Theorem, Confidence Intervals, Hypothesis Testing, and Correlation and Regression.

CAUSE AND EFFECT/ FISHBONE DIAGRAM

Why use it?

Cause & Effect (C&E) Diagrams (also known as Fishbone or Ishikawa Diagrams) allow a team to identify, explore, and graphically display, in increasing detail, important possible causes related to a problem or condition to discover its root cause(s). A C&E Diagram is often used at the start of the Analyze phase of a DMAIC project to help identify which potential root causes to measure.

What does it do?

A C&E Diagram:

- Enables a team to focus on the content of the problem, not on the history of the problem or differing personal interests of team members

- Creates a snapshot of the collective knowledge and consensus of a team around a problem. This builds support for the resulting solutions

- Focuses the team on causes, not symptoms

How do I do it?

1. Select the most appropriate Cause & Effect format. There are two major formats:

   - A dispersion analysis type is constructed by placing individual causes within each "major" cause category and then asking of each individual cause "Why does this cause (dispersion) happen?" This question is repeated for the next level of detail until the team runs out of causes. (The graphic examples shown in step 3 of this section are based on this format.)

- A process classification type uses the major steps of the process in place of the major cause categories. The root cause questioning process is the same as the dispersion analysis type

2. **Generate the causes needed to build a Cause & Effect Diagram, using either:**

- Brainstorming without previous preparation
- Check Sheets based on data collected by team members before the meeting

3. **Construct the Cause & Effect/Fishbone Diagram**

   a) Place the problem statement in a box on the right-hand side of the writing surface

   - Allow plenty of space. Use a flipchart sheet, butcher paper, or a large white board. A paper surface is preferred because the final Cause & Effect Diagram can be moved

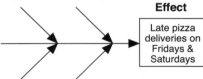

Causes
"Bones"
(Major cause categories)

Effect

Late pizza deliveries on Fridays & Saturdays

Tip Make sure everyone agrees on the problem statement. Include as much information as possible on the "what," "where," "when," and "how much" of the problem. Use data to specify the problem.

b) Draw major cause categories or steps in the production or service process. Connect them to the "backbone" of the fishbone chart

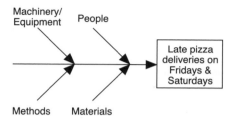

Illustration Note: In a process classification type format, replace the major "bone" categories with: "Order Taking," "Preparation," "Cooking," and "Delivery."

- Be flexible in the major cause "bones" that are used. For a Production Process the traditional categories are: Machines (equipment), Methods (how work is done), Materials (components or raw materials), and People (the human element). For a Service Process the traditional methods are: Policies (higher-level decision rules), Procedures (steps in a task), Plant (equipment and space), and People. In both types of processes, Environment (buildings, logistics, humidity, temperature, and space), and Measurement (calibration and data collection) are also frequently used. There is no perfect set or number of categories. Make them fit the problem

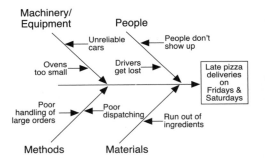

Machinery/
Equipment

People

Unreliable
cars

People don't
show up

Ovens
too small

Drivers
get lost

Late pizza
deliveries
on
Fridays &
Saturdays

Poor
handling of
large orders

Poor
dispatching

Run out of
ingredients

Methods

Materials

c) Place the brainstormed or data-based causes in the appropriate category

- In brainstorming, possible causes can be placed in a major cause category as each is generated, or only after the entire list has been created. Either works well, but brainstorming the whole list first maintains the creative flow of ideas without being constrained by the major cause categories or where the ideas fit in each "bone"

- Some causes seem to fit in more than one category. Ideally each cause should be in only one category, but some of the "people" causes may legitimately belong in two places. Place them in both categories and see how they work out in the end

Tip If ideas are slow in coming, use the major cause categories as catalysts (e.g., "What in 'materials' is causing . . . ?").

d) Ask repeatedly of each cause listed on the "bones," either:

- "Why does it happen?" For example, under "Run out of ingredients," this question would lead to more basic causes, such as "Inaccurate ordering," "Poor use of space," and so on

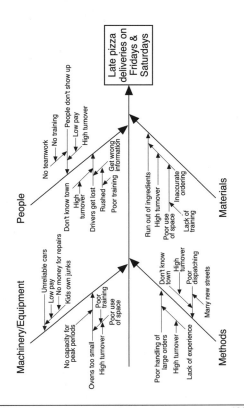

- "What could happen?" For example, under "Run out of ingredients," this question would lead to a deeper understanding of the problem, such as "Boxes," "Prepared dough," "Toppings," and so on

Tip For each deeper cause, continue to push for deeper understanding, but know when to stop. A good practice is to stop questioning when a cause is controlled by more than one level of management removed from the group. Otherwise, the process could become an exercise in frustration.

Tip It is often more helpful to identify the knowledge gap or skills gap rather than pointing to poor training or no procedures.

e) Interpret or test for root cause(s) by one or more of the following:

- Look for causes that appear repeatedly within or across major cause categories

- Select which potential root causes to measure through either an unstructured consensus process or one that is structured, such as Cause & Effect Matrix, Nominal Group Technique, or Multivoting

- Gather data through Check Sheets or other formats to determine the relative frequencies of the different causes

Variations

Traditionally, Cause & Effect Diagrams have been created in a meeting setting. The completed "fishbone" is often reviewed by others and/or confirmed with data collection. An effective alternative is to prominently display a large, highly visible, blank fishbone chart in a work area. Everyone posts both potential causes and solutions on Post-it® Notes in each of the categories. Causes and solutions are reviewed, tested, and posted. This technique opens up the process to the knowledge and creativity of every person in the operation.

Bed Assignment Delay

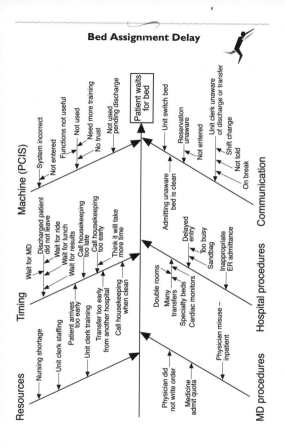

Information provided courtesy of
Rush-Presbyterian-St. Luke's Medical Center

Causes for Bent Pins (Plug-In Side)

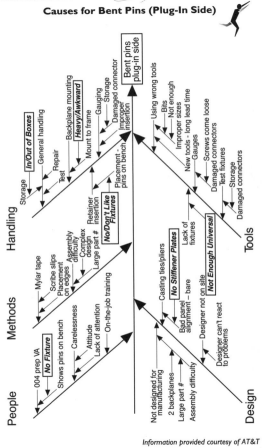

Handling

Storage
General handling
In/Out of Boxes
Repair
Test
Backplane mounting
Heavy/Awkward
Mount to frame
Gauging
Storage
Damaged connector
Improper insertion
Placement - pins on bench
Retainer insertion
Assembly difficulty
Complex design
Large part #
No/Don't Like Fixtures
On-the-job training

Methods

Mylar tape
Scribe slips
Placement on edges
Attitude
Lack of attention
Carelessness

People

004 prep VA
No Fixture
Shows pins on bench

Tools

Using wrong tools
Bits
Not enough
Improper sizes
New tools - long lead time
Gauges
Screws come loose
Damaged connectors
Test fixtures
Storage
Damaged connectors
Lack of fixtures
Not Enough Universal
Casting ties/pliers
No Stiffener Plates
Bad panel alignment – bare
Designer not on site

Design

Not designed for manufacturing
2 backplanes
Large part #
Assembly difficulty
Designer can't react to problems

Bent pins plug-in side

Information provided courtesy of AT&T

© 2018 GOAL/QPC

# GRAPHICAL ANALYSIS

Why use it?

Graphical analysis is an effective way to present data and generate clues. Graphs help you learn from the data, form valid hypotheses, check your assumptions, identify relationships, determine the biggest opportunities, and find anomalies, outliers, shifts, cycles, and trends.

What does it do?

Graphical analysis provides visual techniques that enable you to look at and interpret your data from several perspectives. Graphs allow an organization to represent data (either variable or attribute) to evaluate central tendency and spread, detect patterns in the data, and identify sources of variation in the process.

How do I do it?

1. Formulate the questions you are trying to answer

2. Determine the data you need to answer the questions

3. Create a data collection plan

4. Collect the data and put it into the appropriate format in the graphing software

5. Create appropriate graphs

6. Formulate your findings. If you need objective conclusions, conduct statistical analysis of the data

The type of data collected and your desired perspective will determine the type of graph used to represent the data. This chapter describes some common graphs for different data types.

Histograms

Histograms are an efficient graphical method for describing the distribution of data. However, a large enough sample (greater than 50 data points) is required to effectively show the distribution. Data is divided into groups called bins. The number of data points within a bin is counted and bars are drawn for each bin where the height of the bar represents the count (frequency). The shape of the resultant histogram can be used to assess:

- Measures of central tendency
- Variation in the data
- Shape or underlying distribution of the data (when compared to a normal distribution)

Software packages such as Minitab® are available that will automatically calculate the bin intervals and allow the user to revise them as required. The number of intervals shown can influence the pattern of the sample.

Plotting the data is always recommended. Four unique distributions of data are shown on the following pages. All four data plots share an identical mean, but the spread of the data about the mean differs significantly.

Tip Always look for twin or multiple peaks indicating that the data comes from two or more sources (e.g., machines, shifts, people, or suppliers). If multiple peaks are evident, the data must then be stratified.

Histogram

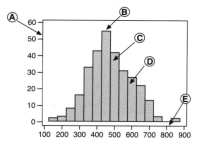

A. The vertical axis shows the frequency or percentage of data points in each class.

B. The modal class is the class with the highest frequency.

C. The frequency is the number of data points found in each class.

D. Each bar is one class or interval.

E. The horizontal axis shows the scale of measure for the Critical To characteristics.

The normal distribution, sometimes referred to as a bell-shaped or Gaussian curve, is an example of a symmetric distribution. Notice that there is a single point of central tendency and the data are symmetrically distributed about the center.

Some processes are naturally skewed. These distributions do not appear normally distributed and may require transformation prior to statistical analysis. Data that sometimes exhibit negative skewness are cash flow, yield, and strength. Data that sometimes exhibit positive skewness are home prices, salaries, cycle time of delivery, and surface roughness.

(For more information on histograms, refer to *The Memory Jogger®2*.)

Chapter 22 - Graphical Analysis   145

Four Distributions of Data

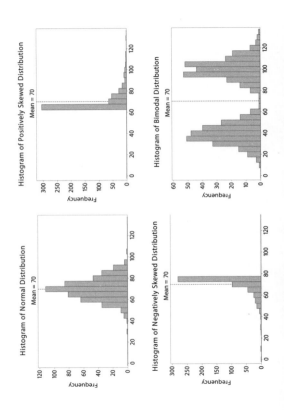

Boxplot

A boxplot (sometimes called a box and whisker plot) can be used to view variability and centering, based on quartiles, in a variable output (y) vs. an attribute input (x) at one or more levels.

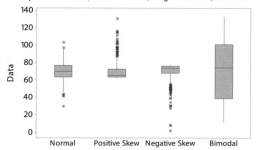

Boxplot of Normal, Positive Skew, Negative Skew, Bimodal

Quartiles rank-order the data and identify the 25th, 50th, and 75th percentiles. The line in the middle of the box represents the median, the line at the bottom of the box represents the first quartile, and the line at the top of the box represents the third quartile. Fifty percent of the data falls within the box.

The Interquartile (IQ) Range is equal to the range between the first and third quartile (Q3 - Q1).

Whiskers are limited by a mathematical calculation. The upper whisker cannot be longer than Q3 + 1.5 x (Q3 - Q1). The whisker line is drawn to the largest value in the data set below this calculated value. If there are data points above this value, they show up as asterisks to indicate they may be outliers. The same is true for the lower whisker with a limit of Q1 - 1.5 x (Q3 - Q1). The whisker line is then drawn to the smallest value in the data set above this calculated value.

Dot Plot

Multiple occurrences are stacked vertically along the x axis. The dot plot is an effective tool for comparing central location and variability within and between factor levels, especially when the sample size is small.

Dotplot of Normal, Positive Skew Negative Skew, Bimodal

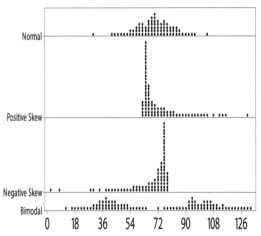

Each symbol represents up to eight observations

The dot plot shows variability in a sample of variable or attribute data. Multiple dot plots can be constructed for discrete levels of another variable.

Individual Value Plot

Note that an Individual Value Plot is similar to a dot plot, with the axes rotated 90 degrees.

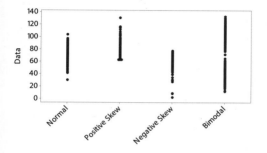

Individual Value Plot of Normal, Positive Skew Negative Skew, Bimodal

Scatter Diagram

The scatter diagram is used to determine whether a qualitative relationship, linear or curvilinear, exists between two continuous or attribute variables. Scatter Diagrams help provide visual evidence of a Cause & Effect Diagram or Matrix to determine if there is more than just a consensus connection between causes and effects.

Scatterplot of Customers vs Suppliers

This scatter diagram shows a strong positive relationship between the number of customers and the number of suppliers; as the number of customers increases, so does the number of suppliers.

Subsequent analysis, such as correlation and regression are typically used to quantify the relationship in a scatter diagram.

Tip The Scatter Diagram does not predict cause and effect relationships; it only shows the strength of the relationship between two variables.

(For more information on Scatter Diagrams, refer to *The Memory Jogger®2*.)

Time Series Plot

Time Series Plots allow a team to study observed data (a performance measure of a process) for trends or patterns over a specified period of time. Generally, 20-25 data points should be collected to detect meaningful patterns.

A Time Series Plot:

- Monitors the performance of one or more processes over time to detect trends, shifts, or cycles

- Allows a team to compare a performance measure before and after implementation of a solution, to measure its impact

- Focuses attention on truly vital changes in the process

- Tracks useful information for predicting trends

If there are no obvious trends, calculate the average or arithmetic mean. The average is the sum of the measured values divided by the number of data points. (The median value can also be used but the mean is the most frequently used measure of the "centering" of the sample.) Draw a horizontal line at the average value.

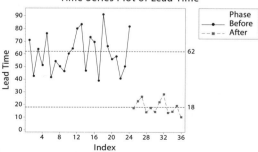

Time Series Plot of Lead Time

Note: The data entry step of the sales process was streamlined after Index 23, making it much simpler for the department staff to process the customer information.

Tip Do not redraw this average line every time new data is added. Only when there has been a significant change in the process or prevailing conditions should the average be recalculated and redrawn, and then only using the data points after the verified change.

Tip A danger in using a Time Series Plot is the tendency to see every variation in data as being important. The Time Series Plot should be used to focus on truly vital changes in the process. Simple tests can be used to look for meaningful trends and patterns. (These tests are found in the "Determining if the Process is Out of Control" section of the Control Charts chapter of this book. Remember that for more sophisticated uses, a Control Chart is invaluable because it is simply a Time Series Plot with statistically based limits.)

Pareto Chart

A Pareto Chart helps focus efforts on the cause categories that offer the greatest potential for improvement by showing their relative frequency or size in a descending bar graph. A Pareto Chart is based on the Pareto Principle: typically 20% of the cause categories are responsible for 80% of the problem.

When setting up a data collection plan for a Pareto Chart, choose the cause categories that will be monitored, compared, and rank-ordered. Choose the most meaningful unit of measurement, such as frequency or cost. Sometimes it is difficult to know before the study is done which unit of measurement is best. Be prepared to do both frequency and cost. Choose a time period that is long enough to represent the situation. Longer studies don't always translate to better information. Look first at volume and variety within the data. Make sure the scheduled time is typical in order to take into account seasonality or even different patterns within a given day or week.

The graphical output from software such as Minitab® shows the cause categories rank-ordered from left to right. The vertical bars represent the relative frequency of each of the cause categories. The cumulative line represents the cumulative percentage of the cause categories. In the example shown here, the first three cause categories (Illegible, Scratch, and Crack) account for 82.5% of the defects.

Pareto Chart of Defect Categories for Mobile Phones

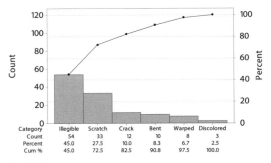

Category	Illegible	Scratch	Crack	Bent	Warped	Discolored
Count	54	33	12	10	8	3
Percent	45.0	27.5	10.0	8.3	6.7	2.5
Cum %	45.0	72.5	82.5	90.8	97.5	100.0

Variations

The Pareto Chart is one of the most widely and creatively used improvement tools. The most frequently used variations of the Pareto Chart are:

A. Major Cause Breakdowns in which the "tallest bar" is broken into subcauses in a second, linked Pareto Chart

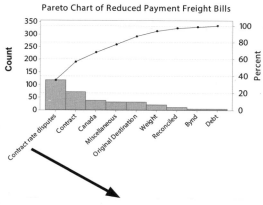

Pareto Chart of Reduced Payment Freight Bills

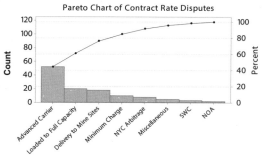

Pareto Chart of Contract Rate Disputes

B. **Before and After** in which the "new Pareto Chart"
bars are drawn side by side with the original Pareto
chart, showing the effect of a change. It can be
drawn as one chart or two separate charts

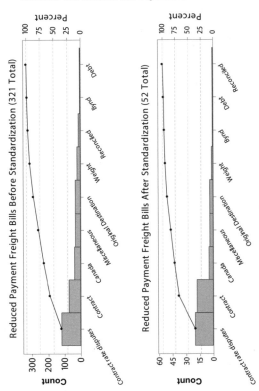

C. Change the Source of Data in which data is collected on the same problem but from different departments, locations, equipment, and so on, and shown in side-by-side Pareto Charts

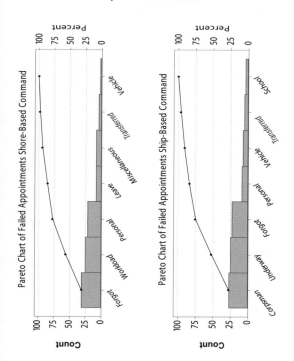

D. Change Measurement Scale in which the same
categories are used but measured differently.
Typically "cost" and "frequency" are alternated

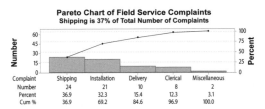

Pareto Chart of Field Service Complaints
Shipping is 37% of Total Number of Complaints

Complaint	Shipping	Installation	Delivery	Clerical	Miscellaneous
Number	24	21	10	8	2
Percent	36.9	32.3	15.4	12.3	3.1
Cum %	36.9	69.2	84.6	96.9	100.0

Pareto Chart of Field Service Complaints
Shipping is 12.5% of Total Cost of Complaints

Complaint	Installation	Clerical	Shipping	Delivery	Miscellaneous
Cost	18000	5000	4000	3000	2000
Percent	56.3	15.6	12.5	9.4	6.3
Cum %	56.3	71.9	84.4	93.8	100.0

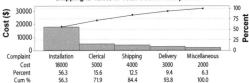

Graphical Summary

Graphical summary is a tool that can be used to
summarize a collection of individual observations
for a continuous variable. Quantitative inferences
about the data set can be made by analyzing the many
statistics that a graphical summary provides. Most
common statistical programs provide some version of
a graphical summary; the following summary comes
from Minitab® software.

Summary Report for Normal

Anderson-Darling Normality Test

A-Squared	0.42
P-Value	0.328

Mean	70.000
StDev	10.000
Variance	100.000
Skewness	-0.050008
Kurtosis	0.423256
N	500

Minimum	29.824
1st Quartile	63.412
Median	69.977
3rd Quartile	76.653
Maximum	103.301

95% Confidence Interval for Mean

69.121	70.879

95% Confidence Interval for Median

69.021	70.737

95% Confidence Interval for StDev

9.416	10.662

95% Confidence Intervals

The data from the graph shows a representative sample of the population. Described below is the information contained in the summary.

A **Section A:** The bell-shaped curve is a normal curve (determined by the average and standard deviation of the data) and assumes normality. The bars in the histogram are the actual data

B **Section B:** Shown to the right of the histogram is the summary information. N is the number of observations. The Anderson-Darling Normality Test is a check for normality. If the p-value is equal to or less than a specified alpha (α) risk, there is evidence that the data does not follow a normal distribution. Because the p-value is greater than 0.05 (the typical α risk), the results of this analysis suggest that the data is normally distributed. Kurtosis is a measure of the heaviness of the tails of the distribution. Departures from zero can indicate non-normality. Positive kurtosis indicates heavier tails than normal (for example, the distribution may look as if it has a high peak and long tails). Negative kurtosis indicates lighter tails (for example, the distribution may look as if it has a flat peak and short tails). This example is very near zero

C **Section C:** This boxplot displays the variability based on rank-ordering the data into quartiles

D **Section D:** The 95% Confidence Interval for Mean is an interval that can be said, with 95% certainty, to contain the true value of the population mean. The 95% Confidence Interval for Median is an interval that can be said, with 95% certainty, to contain the true value of the population median

Normal Probability Plot

A normal probability plot is used to graphically and analytically perform a hypothesis test to determine if the population distribution is normal. It is a plot of calculated normal probabilities vs. a data scale. A best-fit line simulates a cumulative distribution function for the population from which the data is taken. Data that is normally distributed will appear on the plot as a straight line.

One can also interpret the analytical output from an Anderson-Darling Test. If the p-value is less than the α risk, the data is not from a normal distribution.

In the example output on the previous page from Minitab® software, the plotted points fall very close to the best-fit line. In addition, the p-value (0.328) is greater than the α risk (0.05). Therefore, the data in this example is from a normal distribution.

Additional distributions have been plotted as well. Notice the departure of the plotted data from the line for the positive-skewed, negative-skewed, and bimodal distributions. Accordingly, the p-values are less than the α risk, indicating that the data from these distributions may not be from a normal distribution.

Normal Probability Plots

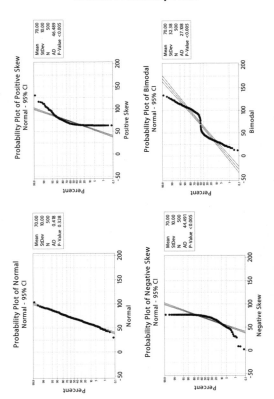

© 2018 GOAL/QPC

Why use it?

If you have a problem of too much variability, a Multi-Vari chart helps to partition the sources of variability so that you can focus on the biggest sources of variability. It also helps identify possible patterns in the data, which may provide some additional clues.

What does it do?

A Multi-Vari chart is a graph that depicts Y metric data versus potential sources of variation, such as:

- Positional (at multiple locations within a part)
- Short-term (part-to-part)
- Long-term (time-to-time)

A Multi-Vari chart presents analysis of variance data in graphical format. The chart displays the means at each factor level for every factor, making it possible to visualize which factors contribute the most variation. It is used most often for processes with a short cycle time.

Types of Variation

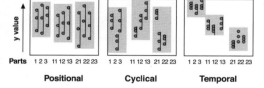

The y axis in this figure records the measure of performance of units taken at different periods of time, in time-order sequence. Each cluster (shaded box)

represents one day, each vertical line represents a consecutive part within each day, and each dot represents a measurement in a different location within each part. Each of the three charts represents a different process, with each process having the greatest source of variation coming from a different component. In the Positional Chart, the greatest variation is within the parts. In the Cyclical Chart, the greatest variation is shown to be between consecutive parts. The Temporal Chart shows the largest variation between the days.

Multi-Vari Example:

In a Multi-Vari study of a sintering process of ceramic tiles, the positional readings of tile thickness were nested within a unit. The positions within each unit were taken at random and were unique to that unit; position 1 on unit A was not the same as position 1 on unit B.

The subgroups of three "consecutive units" were nested within an hour of production. The units inspected were unique to that hour.

A sampling plan, or hierarchy, was created to define the parameters in obtaining samples for the study.

Sampling Plan for a Nested Design

A passive nested study was conducted in which three consecutive units (cyclical) were measured over four hours (temporal). Each unit was measured in three locations, which were randomly chosen on each unit (positional). A Multi-Vari chart was then created to show the results.

Multi-Vari Chart

Multi-Vari Chart for Data by Tile Position - Time

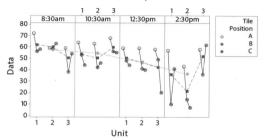

Panel variable: Time

In this example, the time-to-time and position-to-position variability appear to be greater than the unit-to-unit variability. In addition, the variability appears to be increasing over time, and the average values appear to be decreasing over time. The next step in this study would be to evaluate the process parameters that affect time-to-time and position-to-position variation.

How do I do it?

Creating a Multi-Vari Chart?

1. Brainstorm and select potential sources of variation

2. Set up a data collection plan

   • Ensure that your measurement system is acceptable in terms of accuracy, precision, and discrimination

---

3. **Collect the data**

- Collect the data consecutively within each family of variation

- Ensure that the range of the collected data is at least 80% of the historical range

4. **Plot the data in a Multi-Vari chart using software such as Minitab®**

Tip Some computer programs will not produce charts unless the designs are balanced or have at least one data point for each combination.

Tip Each plotted point represents an average of the factor combination selected. When a different order of factors is selected, the data, while still the same, will be re-sorted and the chart will look different. Remember, the order of the hierarchy must be maintained from the top-down or bottom-up of the sampling plan.

5. **Analyze the results**

Ask:

- Is there an area that shows the greatest source of variation?

- Are there cyclic or unexpected nonrandom patterns of variation?

- Are the nonrandom patterns restricted to a single sample or more?

- Are there areas of variation that can be eliminated (e.g., unit-to-unit variation)?

CENTRAL LIMIT THEOREM

Why use it?

The Central Limit Theorem (CLT) is a foundation for parametric hypothesis testing. Understanding this theorem furthers knowledge of how to apply inferential statistics to data.

What does it do?

The Central Limit Theorem states that the means of random samples drawn from *any* distribution with mean μ and variance σ^2 will have an approximately normal distribution with a mean equal to μ and a variance equal to σ^2/n. The CLT allows the use of confidence intervals, hypothesis testing, DOE, regression analysis, and other analytical techniques on data.

Examples:

The CLT can be better understood by reviewing examples of its application. The first example takes samples from a normal distribution; the second and third examples take samples from non-normal distributions. In each case, notice how the sampling distributions are approximately normal. Also notice that as the sample size n increases, the variation decreases and the sampling distribution tends to look more like the normal distribution.

Normal Distribution

Original Population

Normal Distribution

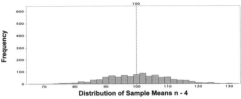

Distribution of Sample Means n - 4

Normal Distribution

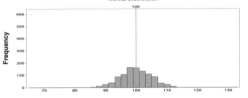

Distribution of Sample Means n - 16

Normal Distribution

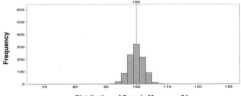

Distribution of Sample Means n - 64

Normal Distribution

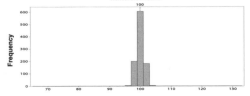

Non-normal Distribution

Original Population
Exponential Distribution

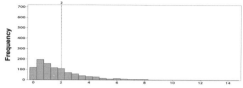

Distribution of Sample Means n - 4
Exponential Distribution

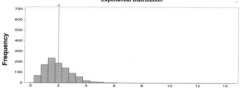

Distribution of Sample Means n - 16
Exponential Distribution

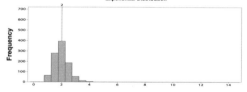

Distribution of Sample Means n - 64
Exponential Distribution

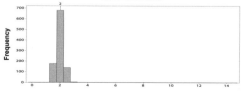

Non-normal Distribution

Original Population
Uniform Distribution

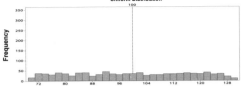

Distribution of Sample Means n - 4
Uniform Distribution

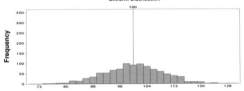

Distribution of Sample Means n - 16
Uniform Distribution

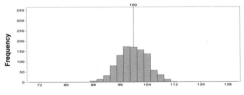

Distribution of Sample Means n - 64
Uniform Distribution

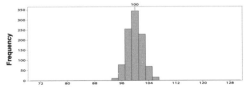

CONFIDENCE INTERVALS

Why use it?

Confidence intervals help to quantify our uncertainty due to random sampling. When we take a sample from a process we use statistics to estimate the location of a population parameter. Because there is variability in these statistical estimates due to random sampling, we need to quantify our uncertainty. Confidence intervals also help us develop the concept of hypothesis testing.

What does it do?

Confidence intervals provide ranges for population parameters (e.g., averages, standard deviations, and proportions) with a certain confidence. When a given population is sampled many times, the calculated sample averages can be different even though the population is stable (as shown in the following figure). Confidence intervals quantify the uncertainty by describing how likely it is that a population parameter lies within a certain range of values. Typically we calculate 95% confidence intervals, meaning we are 95% confident that the population parameter lies within the interval. Conversely, there is a 5% risk (the alpha risk (α) = 1−Confidence = 1−0.95 = 0.05) that the population parameter does not lie within the interval.

Sample Averages

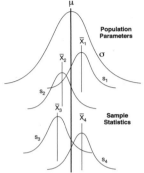

The differences in these sample averages are simply due to the nature of random sampling. Given that these differences exist, the key is to estimate the true population parameter. The confidence interval allows the organization to estimate the true population parameter with a certain confidence.

The confidence interval is bounded by a lower limit and an upper limit that are determined by the risk associated with making a wrong conclusion about the parameter of interest. For example, if the 95% confidence interval is calculated for a subgroup of data of sample size n, and the lower confidence limit and the upper confidence limit are determined to be 85.2 and 89.3, respectively, it can be stated with 95% confidence that the true population average lies between these values. Conversely, there is a 5% risk that this interval does not contain the true population average.

Note:

1. When sampling from a process, the samples are assumed to be randomly chosen and the subgroups are assumed to be independent

2. Whether the true population average lies within the upper and lower confidence limits cannot be known unless we measure the whole population

3. It is extremely rare that we have access to measurements for the whole population. Most statistical packages assume that the data we supply come from a sample

How do I do it?

Depending on the population parameter of interest, the sample statistics that are used to calculate the confidence interval subscribe to different distributions. Aspects of these distributions are used in the calculation of the confidence intervals. Listed below are the different confidence intervals, the distribution the sample statistics subscribe to, the formulas to calculate the intervals, and an example of each. Notice how these confidence intervals are affected by the sample size, n. Larger sample sizes result in tighter confidence intervals, as expected from the Central Limit Theorem. Confidence intervals are also affected by the alpha risk. As we increase the alpha risk (from 5% to 10%, for example) the confidence interval becomes tighter.

Confidence Interval for the Mean

The confidence interval for the mean utilizes a t-distribution and can be calculated using the following formula:

$$\bar{X} - t_{\alpha/2} \left(\frac{s}{\sqrt{n}} \right) \leq \mu \leq \bar{X} + t_{\alpha/2} \left(\frac{s}{\sqrt{n}} \right)$$

Example:

A manufacturer of inserts for an automotive engine application was interested in knowing, with 90% confidence, the average strength of the inserts currently being manufactured. A sample of 20 inserts was selected and tested on a tensile tester. The average strength and standard deviation of these samples were determined to be 167,950 and 3,590 psi, respectively. The confidence interval for the mean μ would be:

$$\overline{X} - t_{\alpha/2}\left(\frac{s}{\sqrt{n}}\right) \leq \mu \leq \overline{X} + t_{\alpha/2}\left(\frac{s}{\sqrt{n}}\right)$$

$$167{,}950 - 1.73\left(\frac{3{,}590}{\sqrt{20}}\right) \leq \mu \leq 167{,}950 + 1.73\left(\frac{3{,}590}{\sqrt{20}}\right)$$

$$167{,}950 - 1{,}389 \leq \mu \leq 167{,}950 + 1{,}389$$

$$166{,}561 \leq \mu \leq 169{,}339$$

Confidence Interval for the Standard Deviation

The confidence interval for the standard deviation subscribes to a chi-square distribution and can be calculated as follows:

$$s\sqrt{\frac{(n-1)}{\chi^2_{\alpha/2,\,n-1}}} \leq \sigma \leq s\sqrt{\frac{(n-1)}{\chi^2_{1-\alpha/2,\,n-1}}}$$

A χ^2 Distribution

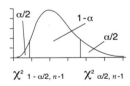

$$\chi^2_{1-\alpha/2,\,n-1} \qquad \chi^2_{\alpha/2,\,n-1}$$

s = standard deviation of a sample
χ^2 = statistical distribution
(values are listed in a statistical table)

Example:

A manufacturer of nylon fiber is interested in knowing, with 95% confidence, the amount of variability in the tenacity (a measure of strength) of a specific yarn fiber they are producing. A sample of 14 tubes of yarn was collected, and the average tenacity and standard deviation were determined to be 2.830 and 0.341 g/denier, respectively. To calculate the 95% confidence interval for the standard deviation:

$$s\sqrt{\frac{(n-1)}{\chi^2_{\alpha/2, n-1}}} \leq \sigma \leq s\sqrt{\frac{(n-1)}{\chi^2_{1-\alpha/2, n-1}}}$$

$$0.341\sqrt{\frac{(14-1)}{24.74}} \leq \sigma \leq 0.341\sqrt{\frac{(14-1)}{5.01}}$$

$$0.247 \leq \sigma \leq 0.549$$

Caution: Some software and texts will reverse the direction of reading the table; therefore, $\chi^2_{\alpha/2, n-1}$ would be 5.01, not 24.74.

Confidence Interval for the Proportion Defective

The exact solution for proportion defective (p) utilizes the binomial distribution; however, in this example the normal approximation will be used. The normal approximation to the binomial may be used when np and n(1-p) are greater than or equal to five. A statistical software package will use the binomial distribution.

$$p - Z_{\alpha/2}\sqrt{\frac{p(1-p)}{n}} \leq P \leq p + Z_{\alpha/2}\sqrt{\frac{p(1-p)}{n}}$$

(This formula is best used when np and n(1-p) > 5.)

Example:

A financial company has been receiving customer phone calls indicating that their month-end financial statements are incorrect. The company would like to know, with 95% confidence, the current proportion defective for these statements. Twelve-hundred statements were sampled and 14 of these were deemed to be defective. The 95% confidence interval for the proportion defective would be:

$$p - Z_{\alpha/2} \sqrt{\frac{p(1-p)}{n}} \le P \le p + Z_{\alpha/2} \sqrt{\frac{p(1-p)}{n}}$$

$$0.012 - 1.96 \sqrt{\frac{0.012(1-0.012)}{1200}} \le P \le 0.012 + 1.96 \sqrt{\frac{0.012(1-0.012)}{1200}}$$

$$0.012 - 0.006 \le P \le 0.012 + 0.006$$

$$0.006 \le P \le 0.018$$

$$0.60\% \le P \le 1.80\%$$

Note: np = 1200 (0.12) = 14.4, which is > 5 and n(1-p) = 1200 (.988) = 1185.6, which is > 5 so the normal approximation to the binomial may be used.

⚡• HYPOTHESIS TESTING

Why use it?

Hypothesis testing helps an organization:

- Determine whether making a change to a process input (x) significantly changes the output (y) of the process

- Statistically determine if there are differences between two or more process outputs

In DMAIC projects, hypothesis testing is used to confirm and quantify root causes in the Analyze phase. It is used in the Improve and Control phases to confirm the effect of the implemented solutions.

What does it do?

Hypothesis testing evaluates two mutually exclusive statements about a population parameter, such as an average, standard deviation, or proportion. These two statements are called the null hypothesis and the alternative hypothesis. They are always statements about population attributes, such as the value of a parameter or the difference between corresponding parameters of multiple populations. A hypothesis test uses sample data to determine which statement is best supported by the data.

Testing a hypothesis using statistical methods is equivalent to quantifying the likelihood of making a wrong decision. When an organization makes a decision based on a statistical test of a hypothesis, it can never be 100% certain whether the decision is right or wrong because of sampling variation. Regardless of how many times the same population is sampled, it will never result in the same sample mean, sample standard deviation, or sample proportion. The real question is whether the differences observed are the result of a real difference in the populations or the result of sampling variation. Statistical tests are used because they have been designed to minimize the probability of making a wrong decision.

There are two basic types of errors that can be made in a statistical test of a hypothesis:

1. A conclusion that the population parameters are different when in fact they are not

2. A conclusion that the population parameters are the same when in fact they are different

The first error is referred to as a type I error. The second error is referred to as a type II error. The probability associated with making a type I error is called alpha (α) or the α risk. The probability of making a type II error is called beta (β) or the β risk.

If the α risk is 0.05, any determination from a statistical test that the population parameters are different runs a 5% risk or being wrong. There is a $1-\alpha$, or 0.95, confidence that the right decision was made.

If the β risk is 0.10, any determination from a statistical test that there is no difference in the population parameters runs a 10% risk of being wrong. There would be a $1-\beta$, or 0.90, "power of the test," which is the ability of the test to detect a difference.

A 5% α risk and a 10% β risk are typical thresholds for the risk DMAIC teams are willing to take when making decisions utilizing statistical tests. Based upon the consequences of making a wrong decision, it is up to the team to determine the risk they want to establish for any given test, in particular the α risk. For example, if there are safety consequences associated with the decision, the team may decide to set the α risk to 0.01 or lower. The β risk, on the other hand, is often determined by the following:

- δ: The difference between the two population parameters. In a DMAIC project, this value is often determined based on what is practically important to achieve the project objective. Holding all other factors constant, as δ increases, β decreases

- σ: The average (pooled) standard deviation of the two populations. Holding all other factors constant, as σ decreases, β decreases

- n: The sample size of each data set. Holding all other factors constant, as n increases, β decreases

- α: The alpha risk or decision criteria. Holding all other factors constant, as α decreases, β increases

Most statistical software packages have Power and Sample Size programs that calculate the proper sample size n to detect a specific δ, given a certain σ and defined α and β risks.

p-Value

How does an organization know if one population parameter is really different from another one, or if an observed difference is merely due to random sampling? Conceptually, all hypothesis tests are the same in that a signal (δ)-to-noise (σ) ratio is calculated (δ/σ) based on the data. This ratio is converted into a probability, called the p-value, which is compared to the decision criteria, the α risk. Comparing the p-value to the decision criteria (the stated α risk) will help determine whether an observed difference is statistically significant. The team must determine whether the observed difference is practically important.

Unfortunately, a decision in a hypothesis test can never conclusively be defined as a correct decision. All the hypothesis test can do is minimize the risk of making a wrong decision.

How do I do it?

Conducting a hypothesis test is analogous to trying a case in a court of law. The objective of the prosecuting attorney is to collect and present enough evidence to prove beyond a reasonable doubt that a defendant is guilty. If the attorney has not done so, then the jury will assume that not enough evidence has been presented to prove guilt; therefore, they will conclude the defendant is not guilty.

A DMAIC team has the same objective. If the team wants to make a change to an input (x) in an existing process to determine a specified improvement in the output (y), they will need to collect data after the change in x to demonstrate beyond some criteria (the α risk) that the specified improvement in y was achieved.

Note: The following steps describe how to conduct a hypothesis test for a difference in means. However, these steps are the same for any hypothesis test on any other population parameter.

1. **Formulate the question you are trying to answer and decide on the appropriate hypothesis test**

2. **Identify the null hypothesis H_0 and the alternative hypothesis H_a**

   - The null hypothesis is a statement of no difference between the before and after states (similar to a defendant being not guilty in court)

   $$H_0: \mu_{before} = \mu_{after}$$

The goal of the test is to either reject or not reject H_0.

3. The alternative hypothesis is what the team is trying to prove and can be one of the following:

$$H_a: \mu_{before} \neq \mu_{after} \text{ (a two-sided test)}$$

$$H_a: \mu_{before} < \mu_{after} \text{ (a one-sided test)}$$

$$H_a: \mu_{before} > \mu_{after} \text{ (a one-sided test)}$$

The alternative chosen depends on what the team is trying to prove. In a two-sided test, it is important to detect differences from the hypothesized mean, μ_{before}, that lie on either side of μ_{before}. The α risk in a two-sided test is split on both sides of the histogram. In a one-sided test, it is only important to detect a difference on one side or the other

4. Determine the practical difference (δ)

   • The practical difference is the meaningful difference the hypothesis test should be able to detect

5. Establish the α risk, β risk, and sample size n based on Power and Sample Size calculations

6. Collect the data, check it for instabilities/outliers, and compare the observed difference to δ

7. Use a software package to analyze the data and determine a p-value. Compare the p-value to the decision criteria (α risk) and determine whether to reject H_0 in favor of H_a, or not to reject H_0

   • If the p-value is less than the α risk, then reject H_0 in favor H_a

   • If the p-value is greater than the α risk, there is not enough evidence to reject H_0

If the observed difference is both practically important and statistically significant, then decide if you may have enough evidence to confirm a root cause and assess its effect or whether you wish to follow up with further tests.

Depending on the population parameter of interest there are different types of hypothesis tests. A software program such as Minitab® can help you select the appropriate test, as depicted in the following graphic.

Hypothesis Test Menu

Continuous data	Compare means	1 sample against a target	1-sample t
		2 independent samples	2-sample t
		2 samples with paired observations	Paired t
		≥ 2 samples (factor levels)	ANOVA
	Compare variances	1 sample against a target	1-variance
		2 samples	2-variance
		≥ 2 samples	Test for equal variances
	Correlate to continuous predictor	1 response against a predictor	Simple linear regression
		1 response against ≥ 2 predictors	Multiple regression
	Compare distribution	1 sample against a normal distribution	Normality test
Attribute data	Compare proportions	1 sample against a target	1-proportion
		2 samples	2-proportion
		≥ 2 samples	Chi-square test
	Compare distribution	1 sample against a target distribution	Chi-square goodness of fit

Note: This graphic depicts parametric tests only. Parametric tests are used when the underlying distribution of the data is known or can be assumed (e.g., the data used for t-testing should subscribe to the normal distribution). Parametric tests are fairly robust to non-normality as long as the sample size is greater than about 20 and there are no instabilities observed in a time series plot of the data. Non-parametric tests are used when there is no assumption of a specific underlying distribution of the data.

The risks associated with making an incorrect decision are described in the following table.

Decision Table

If the decision is:

	H_0	H_a
H_0	*Right Decision*	**α Risk** **Type I Error**
H_a	**β Risk** **Type II Error**	*Right Decision*

If the correct answer is:

2 Sample t-Test Example:

A DMAIC team is interested in determining whether temperature has an impact on the yield of a process. The current process runs at 100°C and results in a nominal yield of 28 kg. The team would like to change the temperature to 110°C with the hope of detecting an increase in output. The null hypothesis is defined as:

$$H_0: \mu_{100°C} = \mu_{110°C}$$

and the alternative hypothesis is chosen as:

$$H_a: \mu_{100°C} < \mu_{110°C}$$

The practical difference the team would like to detect is 3 kg (an increase to 31 kg). The test is conducted with an α and β risk of 5% and 10%, respectively. To achieve a β risk of 10%, twenty-one observations will need to be collected at both 100°C and 110°C; therefore, twenty-one observations were collected at 100°C, the process temperature was changed to 110°C, and twenty-one more observations were collected. The respective averages and standard deviations were 28.2 and 3.2, and 32.4 and 3.2.

The data was entered into a software program and the p-value was determined to be 0.01. After comparing the p-value (0.01) to the α risk (0.05), H_0 is rejected in favor of H_a as there is only a 1% risk in deciding H_a is greater than H_0 when compared to the α risk of 5%. The team concluded that temperature was a significant factor, and that a 10°C increase in temperature causes a 4.2 kg increase in yield.

2 Proportion Test Example:

A team is interested in determining whether a new method of processing forms will result in fewer defective forms. The old method resulted in 5.2% defectives. The team would like to change to a new method with the hope of reducing the percent defectives to 2.0%. The null hypothesis is defined as:

$$H_0: P_{old\ method} = P_{new\ method}$$

and the alternative hypothesis is chosen as:

$$H_a: P_{old\ method} > P_{new\ method}$$

The practical difference the team would like to detect is a 3.2% reduction. The test will be conducted with an α and β risk of 5% and 10%, respectively. To achieve a β risk of 10%, 579 forms will need to be collected using the old and new methods; therefore, 579 forms were collected with the old process, the new method was implemented, and 579 more forms were collected. The respective percentages were 5.2% (thirty defectives) and 2.9% (17 defectives).

The data was entered into a software program and the p-value was determined to be 0.026. Comparing the p-value (0.026) to the α risk (0.05) results in a conclusion that H_0 should be rejected. The team concluded that the new method was significantly better than the old method, but the improvement did not meet their practical goal.

Notes

CORRELATION AND REGRESSION

Correlation

Why use it?

Correlation allows us to identify significant relationships and sources of variability when we have at least two continuous variables. If two variables are correlated and there is a cause-effect relationship, we can then consider using regression analysis to obtain a prediction equation.

What does it do?

Correlation determines whether a linear relationship exists between two continuous variables. It is a hypothesis test where the null hypothesis implies that there is no correlation. Correlation also measures the strength of the relationship (the degree of association) between two independent continuous variables. However, even if there is a high degree of correlation, this tool does not establish causation. For example, the number of skiing accidents in Colorado is highly correlated with sales of warm clothing, but buying warm clothes did not cause the accidents.

How do I do it?

Correlation can be analyzed by calculating the Pearson correlation coefficient. This coefficient is calculated as follows:

$$r_{xy} = \frac{\dfrac{1}{n-1} \sum_{i=1}^{n} (x_i - \bar{X})(y_i - \bar{y})}{S_x S_y}$$

Where S_x and S_y are the sample standard deviations.

The resulting value will be a number between -1 and +1. The higher the absolute value of r, the stronger the correlation. A value of zero means there is no correlation. A strong correlation is characterized by a tight distribution of plotted pairs about a best-fit line. It should be noted that correlation does not measure the slope of the best-fit line; it measures how close the data are to the best-fit line. A negative r implies that as one variable (x) increases, the other variable (y) decreases. A positive r implies that as one variable increases, the other variable also increases. Note that because correlation is a measure of the linear relationship between two variables, a strong curvilinear relationship can exist, yet r can be close to zero.

Examples of Y vs x Relationships

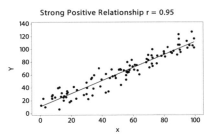

Examples of Y vs x Relationships Cont'd

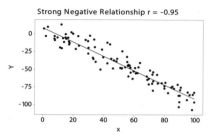

Strong Negative Relationship r = -0.95

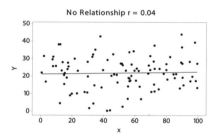

No Relationship r = 0.04

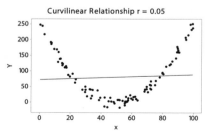

Curvilinear Relationship r = 0.05

Regression

Why use it?

The output of a regression analysis is a prediction equation that allows us to estimate an output Y given an input x or multiple x's. If we find a strong cause-effect relationship, we can make accurate predictions.

What does it do?

In general, regression measures the strength of association between independent factor(s) (also called predictor variable(s) or regressors) and a dependent variable (also called a response variable). For simple or multiple linear regression, the dependent variable must be a continuous variable. Predictor variables can be continuous or attribute, but must be independent of one another. Attribute variables may be coded, discrete levels (dummy variables (0, 1) or effects coding (-1, +1)). There are many types of regression.

Simple linear regression relates a single x to a y. It has a single regressor (x) variable and its model is linear with respect to coefficients (a).

Examples:

$$y = a_0 + a_1x + error$$
$$y = a_0 + a_1x + a_2 x^2 + a_3 x^3 + error$$

Note: "Linear" refers to the coefficients a_0, a_1, a_2, etc. In the second example, the relationship between x and y is a cubic polynomial in nature, but the model is still linear with respect to the coefficients.

Multiple linear regression relates multiple x's to a y. It has multiple regressor (x) variables, such as x_1, x_2, and x_3. Its model is linear with respect to coefficients (b).

Example:

$$y = b_0 + b_1 x_1 + b_2 x_2 + b_3 x_3 + error$$

Other types of regression are best performed by computer programs. Nonlinear regression is applicable when you cannot adequately model the relationship with linear parameters. Logistic regression includes binary logistic regression (which relates x's to a y that can only have a binary value, such as pass/fail, on/off, etc.), ordinal logistic regression (three or more categories with a natural order, such as mild, medium, and hot), and nominal logistic regression (three or more categories of no natural order, such as yellow, blue, and red).

How do I do simple regression?

1. Determine which relationship will be studied

2. Collect data on the x and y variables. For best results, try to collect at least 40 pairs of data

3. Set up a fitted line plot by charting the independent variable on the x axis and the dependent variable on the y axis

4. Create the fitted line

   - If creating the fitted line plot by hand, draw a straight line through the values that keep the least amount of total space between the line and the individual plotted points (a "best fit")

   - If using a computer program, compute and plot this line via the "least squares method"

Fitted Line Plot

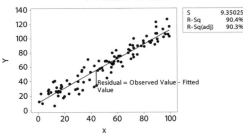

Fitted Line Plot
Y = 11.07 + 1.012 x

S	9.35025
R-Sq	90.4%
R-Sq(adj)	90.3%

Residual = Observed Value - Fitted Value

5. Compute the correlation coefficient r, using the equation defined earlier in this chapter

6. Determine the slope or y intercept of the line by using the equation y = mx + b

   - The y intercept (b) is the point on the y axis through which the "best fitted line" passes (at this point, x = 0)

   - The slope of the line (m) is computed as the change in y divided by the change in x (m = Δy/Δx). The slope, m, is also known as the coefficient of the predictor variable, x

7. Calculate the residuals

   - The difference between the predicted response variable (called the fits, $\hat{y}$) for any given x and the experimental value or actual response (y) is called the residual (e = y - $\hat{y}$). The residual is used to determine if the model is a good one to use. The estimated standard deviation of the residuals is a measure of the error term about the regression line

8. To determine significance, perform a t-test (with the help of a computer) and calculate a p-value for each factor

   - A p-value less than α (usually 0.05) will indicate a statistically significant relationship

9. Analyze the entire model for significance using ANOVA, which displays the results of an F-test with an associated p-value

10. Calculate R^2 and R^2_{adj}

   - R^2, the coefficient of determination, is the square of the correlation coefficient and measures the proportion of variation that is explained by the model. Ideally, R^2 should be equal to one, which would indicate zero error

   $$R^2 = SS_{regression} / SS_{total}$$
   $$= (SS_{total} - SS_{error}) / SS_{total}$$
   $$= 1 - [SS_{error} / SS_{total}]$$

   Where SS = the sum of the squares.

   - R^2_{adj} is a modified measure of R^2 that takes into account the number of terms in the model and the number of data points

   $$R^2_{adj} = 1 - [SS_{error} / (n-p)] / [SS_{total} / (n-1)]$$

   Where n = number of data points and p = number of terms in the model. The number of terms in the model also includes the constant.

   Note: Unlike R^2, R^2_{adj} can become smaller when added terms provide little new information and as the number of model terms gets closer to the total sample size. Ideally, R^2_{adj} should be maximized and as close to R^2 as possible.

Conclusions should be validated, especially when historical data has been used.

Example:

A DMAIC team wants to determine if there is a relationship between the amount of shelf space allocated for a specific product and the sales volume for that same product. They investigate 50 different stores of the same chain, all with similar demographics. Data is collected comparing shelf space allocated (x) to sales (y). Using a computer program to run a regression analysis with ANOVA shows the following result:

Analysis of Variance

```
Regression Analysis: Sales $ versus Shelf Space

The regression equation is
Sales $ = 498.3 + 26.19 Shelf Space


S = 263.642   R-Sq = 87.8%   R-Sq(adj) = 87.6%


Analysis of Variance

Source      DF      SS          MS        F      P
Regression   1   24038891   24038891   345.85  0.000
Error       48    3336341      69507
Total       49   27375231
```

Correlation analysis shows a strong positive correlation ($r = +0.937$). The team concluded that about 88% of the variability in the sales dollars could be attributed to the variability of shelf space. Adding one unit of shelf space corresponded to about $26.00 of additional sales.

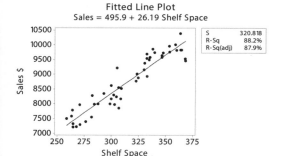

Fitted Line Plot
Sales = 495.9 + 26.19 Shelf Space

S	320.818
R-Sq	88.2%
R-Sq(adj)	87.9%

How do I do more advanced techniques, such as multiple regression and residual analysis?

Using a computer program, a similar method is used to perform multiple regression, but the x axis can no longer represent a single factor.

1. After obtaining a prediction equation (y = mx + b), analyze the residuals to validate the assumptions for regression

   Residuals should:

   - Be normally distributed with a mean of zero

   - Show no pattern (i.e., be random)

   - Have constant variance when plotted against any regression factor or predicted values fits

- Be independent of the predictor variables (x's)
- Be independent of each other

2. **Check for patterns**
   - Any significant pattern seen may be an indication of a missed factor. Add extra factors, try a quadratic multiplier, modify the formula, or transform the data and reanalyze the model

3. **Once any patterns are eliminated, confirm that multicollinearity is minimized**
   - Multicollinearity is a measure of correlation between the independent variables and can be quantified with the Variation Inflation Factor. (Ideally, VIF < 5.) (More detail about VIF goes beyond the scope of this book. For detailed information, see *Introduction to Linear Regression Analysis* by D.C. Montgomery and E.A. Peck)

4. **Calculate R^2 and R^2_{adj}**

Tip Make sure that the R^2_{adj} is the highest value obtainable with the fewest (simplest model) number of variables. Best subsets and stepwise regression are methodologies that help this optimizing effort.

Example:

A DMAIC team wants to evaluate the effect of three continuous factors (temperature, pressure, and dwell) on the yield of a process.

Data from 50 runs is collected and, as shown in the table, all three factors are statistically significant, giving a regression formula of four terms. This computer-generated output provides the ANOVA table and p-values, confirming the validity of our model (F-test) and its component factors (t-tests).

ANOVA and p-Values

Regression Analysis: Yield versus Temperature, Pressure, Dwell

Analysis of Variance

Source	DF	Adj SS	Adj MS	F-Value	P-Value
Regression	3	333.61	111.203	97.01	0.000
Temperature	1	16.74	16.738	14.60	0.000
Pressure	1	52.00	51.999	45.36	0.000
Dwell	1	263.26	263.261	229.67	0.000
Error	46	52.73	1.146		
Total	49	386.34			

Model Summary

S	R-sq	R-sq(adj)	R-sq(pred)
1.07063	86.35%	85.46%	83.87%

Coefficients

Term	Coef	SE Coef	T-Value	P-Value	VIF
Constant	-0.71	3.08	-0.23	0.818	
Temperature	0.1633	0.0427	3.82	0.000	1.03
Pressure	0.2869	0.0426	6.74	0.000	1.01
Dwell	0.11324	0.00747	15.15	0.000	1.02

Regression Equation

Yield = -0.71 + 0.1633 Temperature + 0.2869 Pressure + 0.11324 Dwell

The residuals were analyzed to validate the assumptions for regression/ANOVA.

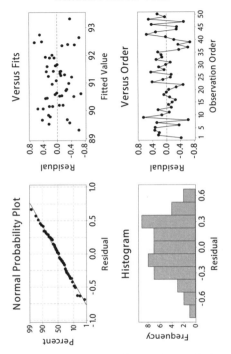

Some computer programs will scan the residuals and identify any standardized residual over a set limit (typically two). This is essentially an identification of potential outliers possibly worth investigating.

Note that a Standardized Residual = Residual ÷ Standard Deviation of the Residual.

# IMPROVE PHASE

The purpose of the Improve phase is to improve the process by implementing solutions that address the root causes that were confirmed in the Analyze phase. The major deliverables include:

- A list of potential solutions
- A list of confirmed solutions
- A revised process map
- A risk analysis, such as an FMEA (Failure Mode and Effects Analysis)
- An implementation plan
- Pilot results

When the Improve phase is complete, solutions have been implemented and proven to fix the problem on a pilot basis. The team is then prepared to proceed to the Control phase to put controls in place to maintain the gains.

In the Improve phase, the major tasks are to:

- Identify potential solutions to the root causes proven in the Analyze phase
- Select and confirm solutions using tests, such as hypothesis tests and designed experiments
- Revise the process map and manage risk using a tool such as FMEA
- Prepare an implementation plan
- Pilot the solutions, check the results, and adjust as necessary

IMPROVE

Step	Tools	Outputs
Identify potential solutions	Brainstorming, idea generation	List of potential solutions
Select and confirm solutions	Solution Selection, Prioritization Matrix, Force Field Analysis, Designed Experiments	Confirmed solutions
Revise process map and manage risk	Process Mapping, Failure Mode and Effects Analysis (FMEA)	Risk management plan for revised process
Prepare implementation plan	Implementation plan	Implementation plan, communication plan
Pilot solutions, check results	Piloting Solutions, PDCA	Piloted solutions and proven short-term results

The chapters in this section include Solution Selection, Failure Mode and Effects Analysis, and Piloting Solutions. Hypothesis testing, process mapping, and preparing project plans are covered in earlier chapters. Designed experiments are covered in *The Black Belt Memory Jogger® Second Edition*.

 SOLUTION SELECTION

Why use it?

In the Improve phase, solution selection is an efficient way to generate solution ideas and select the best solutions to address the root causes proven in the Analyze phase. Following the solution selection process builds stakeholder support for solutions.

What does it do?

Solution selection is a set of techniques to decide which solutions to pursue in the Improve phase. The input is a list of proven root causes, and the output is a list of selected solutions.

How do I do it?

1. Review the list of proven root causes

2. Generate a list of potential solutions, using insights from the Analyze phase, benchmarking, brainstorming, or other tools that can be found in *The Creativity Tools Memory Jogger®*

3. Narrow the list of potential solutions by removing obvious misfits, such as ideas that may:

   - Adversely affect customers
   - Directly conflict with the organization's strategy or core values
   - Violate a law or company policy
   - Exceed the scope of the charter

4. **Set up a solution selection matrix, which is a special version of a prioritization matrix:**

    A. Determine the selection criteria, such as effectiveness of the solution, cost of implementation, ease of implementation, time to implement, risk, etc.

    B. Weight the relative importance of each criterion to the customer

    C. List the remaining potential solutions

    D. Rate the degree to which each solution satisfies each criterion

    E. Calculate total weighted scores for the solutions and prioritize them

5. **Use Force Field Analysis to optimize the highest ranked solutions before presenting them to the project sponsor for approval:**

   - Describe the proposed solution

   - Brainstorm driving forces that currently work in favor of the solution, such as resources, experiences, attitudes, sponsorship, etc.

   - Brainstorm restraining forces that currently hinder the solution

   - Review the restraining forces and determine if you can eliminate or minimize them

   - Review the driving forces and determine if you can enhance them or offset any restraining forces

   - Prepare an action plan to optimize the proposed solution based on this analysis

---

Example

A team is working on a project to reduce the elapsed time to repair customer equipment. They found three root causes in the Analyze phase. The team used brainstorming to create a long list of potential solutions to address the three root causes.

List of Potential Solutions

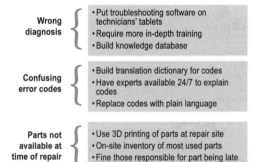

Wrong diagnosis	• Put troubleshooting software on technicians' tablets • Require more in-depth training • Build knowledge database
Confusing error codes	• Build translation dictionary for codes • Have experts available 24/7 to explain codes • Replace codes with plain language
Parts not available at time of repair	• Use 3D printing of parts at repair site • On-site inventory of most used parts • Fine those responsible for part being late

The team decided to remove one potential solution, "Fine those responsible for part being late", because it was a misfit in terms of conflicting with the company's core values.

The team followed the procedure to create a solution selection matrix. They decided to pursue the top three prioritized solutions.

The team then created a Force Field Analysis for the top solution to optimize it before presenting it to the project sponsor.

Example Solution Selection Matrix

B. Weight the relative importance of each criterion to the customer →	10	8	3	5	E. Prioritize on total score↓
A. List criteria for selecting solutions →	Effectiveness	Time	Cost	Risk	
C. List potential solutions ↓	D. Rate the degree to which each solution satisfies each criterion↓				
Put troubleshooting software on tablets	9	3	5	3	144
On-site inventory of most used parts	5	5	3	9	144
Build translation dictionary for codes	5	5	3	5	124
Replace codes with plain language	9	0	3	5	124
Use 3D printing of parts at repair site	9	0	0	1	95
Have experts available 24/7 to explain codes	5	3	1	3	92
Build knowledge database	5	1	5	3	88

Example Force Field Analysis

Force Field Analysis	
Desired change/solution: Put troubleshooting software on tablets	
Driving forces →	**← Restraining forces**
Strong sponsor support	Initial frustration with new way of working
Higher customer satisfaction	Initially more work for technicians as they start the learning curve
Fewer complaints	Bugs to work out in the new software
Less job stress for technicians	Long IT response times

Action plan:
1. Have sponsor communicate face-to-face with technicians to show support
2. Manage expectations of technicians and keep them informed
3. Monitor lead times & customer satisfaction to make improvements visible
4. Provide a short-term hotline to IT until all the bugs are worked out

FAILURE MODE AND EFFECTS ANALYSIS

Why use it?

Failure Mode and Effects Analysis (FMEA) allows an assessment of the risk to customers if a key process input (x) were to fail. The FMEA also helps to determine what actions to take to minimize this risk. FMEAs are also used to document processes and process improvement activities. In the Improve phase, FMEAs improve the chances of success of the proposed solutions, increase the effectiveness of implementation, and increase stakeholder buy-in.

Note: There are a number of different FMEAs including design, systems, product, and process FMEAs. This chapter describes process FMEAs.

What does it do?

The FMEA provides a documented summary of the team's thoughts regarding risk to the customer if any of the key process inputs to the process fails. The FMEA identifies failure modes associated with the steps of the new process, assesses the effects of those failure modes, and prioritizes the risks. Furthermore, the FMEA contains the recommended and implemented actions to minimize this risk. It is a living document that must be reviewed and updated whenever the process has been modified.

How do I do it?

The initial information needed for an FMEA includes a list of the Key Process Input Variables (x's) determined in the Analyze phase, a list of the proposed solutions identified in the Improve phase, and a revised process map of the proposed process.

1. Include information to identify who completed the form, when the form was completed, and what process the form represents

2. List the process step and the key process input (x). You may wish to focus on the process steps that may be affected by the proposed solutions

3. List the potential failure modes for this key process input. (Note: There may be more than one failure mode.) Describe the failure mode(s) in physical or technical terms, not as a symptom (effect) noted by the customer

4. If the key process input (x) fails, list the effect that the customer experiences. For example, if a fitting on a brake hose was not properly adjusted, the customer would experience "loss of brake pressure"

5. List the potential cause(s) for this failure mode. There may be more than one cause per failure mode. Also consider operating conditions, usage or in-service, and possible combinations as potential causes

6. List the controls that are currently in place to prevent or detect the cause of the failure mode

7. On a scale of 1-10, rate the severity of the failure effect the customer experiences

8. On a scale of 1-10, determine how often the cause of the failure mode occurs

9. On a scale of 1-10, determine how effective the current controls can detect or prevent the cause of the failure mode. If a good detection or prevention system (such as an automated feedback system) is in place, assign a 1 or 2 to this column. If no controls are in place, assign a 10 to this column

Note: A typical rating system for severity, occurrence, and detection is shown in the following figure. The team should agree on this rating system or create one that is more meaningful to their own situation.

FMEA Ratings

Rating	Severity	Occurrence	Detection
10	May endanger without warning	>10%	Impossible to detect
9	May endanger with warning	5%-10%	Very remote likelihood to detect
8	Shut down process	2%-5%	Remote likelihood to detect
7	Slow down process	1%-2%	Very low likelihood to detect
6	100% rework	0.2%-1%	Low likelihood to detect
5	Significant rework	0.05%-0.2%	Moderate likelihood to detect
4	Minor rework	0.01%-0.05%	High likelihood to detect
3	Inconvenience	0.001%-0.01%	Total detection of failure mode
2	Noticeable but no adverse effect	<0.001%	Total prevention of failure mode
1	No effect	Never	Total prevention of cause

10. Multiply the severity, occurrence, and detection ratings together to calculate a risk priority number (RPN). The highest possible RPN would be 1000 and the lowest RPN would be 1. Low values indicate lower risk. The RPN is one indicator to help prioritize recommended actions in the action plan. If, however, any risks have a severity rating of 9 or 10, efforts should first focus on these issues to ensure detection is at most a 1 or 2 and occurrence is also a low number

11. Use the RPN to determine what recommended action will be taken to minimize risk to the customer

   Note: Recommended actions can only affect detection and occurrence ratings. The severity rating can only be changed in rare circumstances. If a high severity rating is observed, consider speaking to the process designers to determine if this key process input can be designed out of the process.

12. After the assigned person has completed the recommended actions, list the specific actions taken, along with the actual completion date. Based on the completed actions, reevaluate the severity (which rarely changes), occurrence, and detection ratings to calculate a new risk priority **number**. Determine if more actions are necessary to reduce the risk further

Current controls from the FMEA should be noted in the initial control plan. The FMEA needs to be updated before handing off the process to the process owner to reflect the completed project. The final FMEA will be used to finalize the control plan. If changes are made to the process in the future, the FMEA will need to be reviewed and updated.

Example:

A DMAIC team was working on a project to reduce the lead time to repair medical equipment. In the Improve phase, they decided to implement a troubleshooting guide on the technicians' tablets. One of the process steps affected by this solution was to search for symptoms in the troubleshooting guide. A key input variable is a complete list of clearly described symptoms. Part of the FMEA that the team created is shown on the following page.

FMEA — Process: On-site field repair process — Date: 15-Feb — Project leader: Tim

Process step / key input variable	Failure mode	Effect	Severity	Cause	Occurrence	Current controls	Detection	RPN	Action plan Actions	Responsibility	Date	Action results Actions taken	Severity 2	Occurrence 2	Detection 2	RPN2
Technician searches for symptom in the troubleshooting guide	May not select the correct symptom	May take longer than it currently does to make the correct repair	5	Symptoms may not be described clearly	5	None	10	250	Hire a technical editor to clarify the symptom descriptions	Ann	1-Mar	Hired editor 2/22 edited symptom descriptions; also set up monthly review to re-edit descriptions based on feedback	5	3	3	45
Technician searches for symptom in the troubleshooting guide	Symptom may not be listed	May take longer than it currently does to make the correct repair	5	Team did not include all possible symptoms	3	Met with technicians and specialists and described symptoms for all documented repairs in last 5 years	3	45	Monitor process during pilot to ensure that all symptoms are covered	Tim	1-Apr	In process				

Notes

PILOTING SOLUTIONS

Why use it?

In the Improve phase, pilots reduce risk and improve the probability of success of solutions by implementing the new process on a small scale, testing the solutions, and performing adjustments to optimize their effectiveness. Pilots help test if the organization is ready for the solutions, and they build support for the new process by involving stakeholders and getting their feedback.

What does it do?

Piloting is the trial implementation of all or part of the proposed solutions on a reduced scale. The basic methodology behind a pilot is the Plan Do Check Act (PDCA) cycle. A typical implementation will go through two or more turns of the PDCA cycle—from small-scale to large-scale pilots. The input is an implementation plan of the proposed solutions, and the output is verified short-term performance that meets the goals set in the Define phase.

How do I do it?

1. Create a pilot plan:

    *   Who will be involved, what resources will need training, and what will be communicated

    *   What will be the scope of the testing, what solutions will be tested, and what materials, equipment, and information will be required

    *   When will the pilots take place and how long will they last

    *   Where will the pilots take place

- How will the pilots be conducted and how will data be collected and analyzed

2. Define the success criteria:
   - The effectiveness of the solutions, i.e., the effect of the solutions on the primary and secondary metrics (did we meet the project goals?)
   - The efficiency of implementation, i.e., the extent to which the organization adopts the new solutions (how well did training and communication prepare stakeholders to adopt the new ways of working?)

3. Conduct a risk assessment and prepare contingency plans

4. Execute the pilot plan and communicate often to manage expectations

5. Check the results:
   - Compare the results against the success criteria
   - Check for any unintended consequences in areas outside the immediate pilot location

6. Act to standardize successes and capture lessons learned by the team

7. Depending on the extent to which the success criteria were met, adjust the solutions and run another small-scale pilot, run a larger-scale pilot, or confirm the short-term performance and proceed to the Control phase

Example Pilot Plan

Pilot Plan		
Who	Resources	Field technicians, Supervisors, Project team members
	Training	Four-hour classroom training on how to use troubleshooting program
	Communication	Initial communication to all Stakeholders, Weekly updates during pilot, Final report
What	Scope	Small-scale in just one zone
	Solutions	Troubleshooting program on tablets
	Materials/ Information	Tablets with troubleshooting software installed
When	Start Date	1-Mar
	Duration	One month
Where	Locations	Zone 1 (greater New York area)
	Departments	Zone 1 Technical Repair Department
How	Procedures	New standard operating procedures documented in troubleshooting program
	Data Collection	Project team members will collect data on lead time to repair equipment, customer satisfaction, frequency of mistakes, technician feedback
Success Criteria	Effectiveness of Solutions	Lead time to repair should decrease from 4 hours to 2.5 hours
	Efficiency of Implementation	Customer satisfaction should not decrease, Frequency of mistakes should decrease from 0.15 to 0.05 mistakes per visit, Technician satisfaction should be at least 4 on a 1-5 scale
Risk Assessment	Major Risks	Troubleshooting software may not work properly
	Contingency Plans	Have expert technicians ready to intervene if necessary
Results	Effectiveness of Solutions	Lead time to repair decreased to 2.7 hours
	Efficiency of Implementation	All measures were met
	Learnings	Training should have included more time to learn how to recognize symptoms
Act	Standardizations	Standardize software and procedures
	Adjustments	Revise training to include more on how to recognize symptoms
	Next Steps	Run larger scale pilot in Zones 1-3

Notes

⋙ CONTROL PHASE

The purpose of the Control phase is to maintain the gains that were verified on a pilot basis in the Improve phase. The major deliverables include:

- Implemented permanent controls

- A standardized control plan

- Confirmed long-term stability and capability performance measures that meet the project goals

- Validated customer satisfaction

- Final project benefit assessment

- Final project documentation

When the Control phase is complete, measures are in place to maintain the gains for the long term and the project is closed out.

In the Control phase, the major tasks are to:

- Implement permanent controls, such as control charts, mistake proofing, visual management, and total productive maintenance

- Standardize the control plan to maintain the gains for the long term

- Confirm long-term stability and capability using control charts and capability analysis

- Validate customer satisfaction and project benefits

- Close out the project

CONTROL		
Step	**Tools**	**Outputs**
Implement permanent controls	Mistake Proofing, Statistical Process Control (SPC)	Process controls
Standardize control plan	Control Plan	Control plan
Confirm improved stability and capability	SPC, Process Capability	Confirmed long-term process performance
Validate customer satisfaction and project benefits	Customer interviews, surveys, project benefits analysis	Validated customer satisfaction and project benefits
Close project	Project review and closure	Completed project documentation

The chapters in this section include Control Charts and Control Plans. Process capability, project benefit assessment, and project close-out procedures are covered in earlier chapters. Total Productive Maintenance is covered in *The Black Belt Memory Jogger® Second Edition*. Mistake Proofing (error proofing) and Visual Management are covered in *The Lean Enterprise Memory Jogger®*.

 **CONTROL CHARTS**

Why use it?

Control Charts are used to monitor, control, and improve process performance over time by studying variation and its source. They help focus attention on detecting special sources of variation. They help improve a process to perform consistently and predictably for higher quality, lower cost, and higher effective capacity. They provide a common language for discussing process performance over time.

What does it do?

A Control Chart:

- Analyzes time-series data and detects special-cause variation through non-random patterns known as "out-of-control" signals. These signals do not tell why the process is out of control, but they do indicate that something unusual occurred that is worth investigating. Out-of-control signals are based on the probability of observing certain events or patterns in random time-series data (such as an observation that falls more than ±3 short-term standard deviations from the mean)

- Helps prevent unnecessary process adjustments. Unnecessary process adjustments just add more noise and waste our efforts. When there are no out-of-control signals, we know that only common-cause variability is present and we should not adjust the process because it is "in control"

- Signals opportunities for improvement. When the control chart gives an out-of-control signal we know special cause variability may have changed the process and we can then take actions to correct the situation

How do I do it?

There are many types of Control Charts. The Control Chart(s) that a team decides to use will be determined by the type of data and subgroup size.

The Tree Diagram

This Tree Diagram of the most common control charts will help to determine which Control Chart will best fit each particular situation.

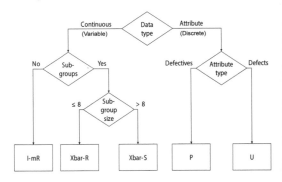

Constructing Control Charts

1. Select the process variable to be charted

2. Determine the sampling method and plan

   • To determine subgroup size, balance the time and cost to collect a sample with the amount of information that will be gathered. For Attribute Data Control Charts the subgroup size times the average proportion defectives or defect rate should be at least 0.5 (e.g., if the average proportion defectives for a P Chart is 0.01, then the subgroup size should be at least 50). For Variable Data Control Charts the subgroup size times the number of subgroups should be at least 100 (e.g., if you collect 20 subgroups of data for an Xbar-R chart, the subgroup size should be at least 5)

- As much as possible, obtain the data within a subgroup under the same technical conditions (the same machine, operator, lot, and so on) so that only common-cause variability is captured within the subgroup

- Frequency of sampling depends on how often you need to be able to detect changes to the process in a timely manner. Consider hourly, daily, shifts, monthly, lots, and so on. Once the process is "in control," consider reducing the frequency with which samples are chosen

- Depending on the subgroup size considerations above, collect 20–100 subgroups. Statistical software programs such as Minitab® will alert you if you should collect more data

Tip Make sure samples are random. To establish the inherent variation of a process, allow the process to run untouched (i.e., according to standard procedures).

3. Collect the data and input it into a statistical software program

4. Have the statistical software program calculate the statistics and construct the control chart

5. Once you have verified that the process is stable (in control), lock the control limits in place and continue monitoring

---

6. Develop an Out-of-Control Action Plan (OCAP) that describes what to do if the process goes out of control (how to identify the special cause, what to do with products made during the out-of-control period, what to do to bring the process back into control, and how to verify that it is back in control)

Interpreting Control Charts

- Attribute Data Control Charts provide one chart per set of data. P Charts and U Charts measure variation between subgroups. If the variation is more or less than expected according to statistical considerations, the software will alert you to use a Laney P' or U' Chart which will adjust the control limits to compensate

- Variable Data Control Charts provide two charts per data set: the top chart (for averages or individuals) measures variation between subgroups over time; the bottom chart (for ranges, standard deviations, or moving ranges) measures variation within subgroups over time. For Variable Data Control Charts, check the bottom chart first to determine if the process variation is stable. If it is not stable, the top chart may not be valid

- Analyze the data relative to the control limits; the statistical software will distinguish between common causes and special causes by flagging out-of-control conditions. Random variation inherent in the process results from common causes within the system (e.g., design, choice of machine, preventive maintenance) and can only be affected by changing that system. However, points outside of the control limits or non-random patterns come from special causes (e.g., human errors, unplanned events, freak occurrences) that are not part of the way the process normally operates. Special causes must be eliminated from the process before the Control Chart can be used as a monitoring tool. Once this is done, the process will be "in control" and samples can be taken at regular intervals to make sure that the process doesn't fundamentally change. (See the "Determining if the Process is Out of Control" section of this chapter)

- A process is "in statistical control" if the process is not being affected by special causes. All the points must fall within the control limits and they must be randomly dispersed for the process to be in control

Tip "In Control" doesn't necessarily mean that the product or service will meet the customer needs. It only means that the process is stable and consistent. Don't confuse control limits with specification limits. Control limits are calculated from the variation in the data, while specification limits are related to customer requirements, not process variation.

Tip Do not remove any out-of-control data from the calculations unless you know the special cause of the instability and have eliminated it. Points within the control limits, but showing indications of trends, shifts, or instability, are also special causes.

Tip When a Control Chart has been initiated and all special causes removed, continue to plot new data on a new chart, but DO NOT recalculate the control limits. As long as the process does not change, the limits should not be changed. Control limits should be recalculated only when a permanent, desired change has occurred in the process, and only using data after the change occurred.

Tip Nothing will change just because a chart was created! An action must occur. Form a team to investigate issues, such as changes in measurement systems, methods, machines, personnel, materials, environmental conditions, or process adjustments.

Chapter 33 - Control Charts   221

Determining if the Process is Out of Control

A process is said to be "out of control" if either one of these is true:

1. One or more points fall outside of the control limits*

2. When the Control Chart is divided into zones indicating the number of short-term standard deviations from the mean, as shown below, any of the following non-random patterns occur:

- - - - - - - - -	Upper Control Limit (UCL)
Zone A	
Zone B	
Zone C	
Zone C	Average
Zone B	
Zone A	
- - - - - - - - -	Lower Control Limit (LCL)

   a) Two out of three consecutive points are on the same side of the average in Zone A or beyond⁺

   b) Four out of five consecutive points are on the same side of the average in Zone B or beyond⁺

   c) Nine consecutive points are on one side of the average*

   d) There are six consecutive points, increasing or decreasing*

   e) There are fourteen consecutive points that alternate up and down*

   f) There are fifteen consecutive points within Zone C (above and below the average)⁺

   *Applies to both variable and attribute data
   ⁺Applies to variable data only

Note that statistical software programs allow you to check for any or all of these out-of-control signals.

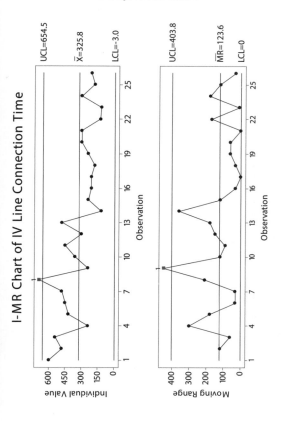

Example I-MR Chart

I-MR Chart of IV Line Connection Time

Individual Value

UCL=654.5
X̄=325.8
LCL=-3.0

Moving Range

UCL=403.8
M̄R=123.6
LCL=0

Observation

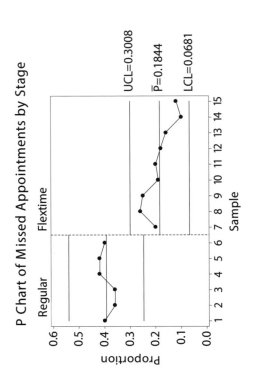

P Chart of Missed Appointments by Stage

Example Xbar-R Chart

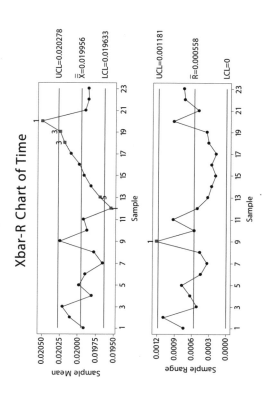

Xbar-R Chart of Time

Example U Chart

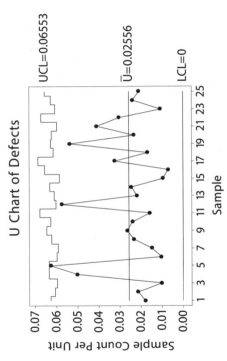

U Chart of Defects

UCL=0.06553

Ū=0.02556

LCL=0

Sample Count Per Unit

Sample

Tests are performed with unequal sample sizes.

CONTROL PLAN

Why use it?

A control plan provides an institutional memory of the status of a process and the measurements that define it. It provides for timely process troubleshooting and repair, and aids in training and audit activities. It becomes a living document within the process to sustain process improvements. It also documents the control activities of a DMAIC project prior to completion.

What does it do?

A DMAIC project control plan is a set of documents that:

- Provides a point of reference among instructions, characteristics, and specifications

- Links Critical to Satisfaction (CTS) characteristics to the operational details of the process

- Encompasses several process areas including operating procedures, preventive maintenance, and gauge control (MSA)

- Provides prevention against process drift or deviation through identified measurement methods and responsibilities as well as out-of-control action plans (OCAPs)

- Empowers local control of process corrective actions and resources

- Can provide shutdown and/or quarantine activities

- Links Key Process Input Variables (KPIVs) to Key Process Output Variables (KPOVs)

- Ensures that a DMAIC project is ready for completion. If a control plan cannot be completed, at least one of the key elements (identification, specification, measurement, planned response to nonconformity, or control/responsibility) has not been defined or agreed

How do I do it?

Determine what controls are necessary to maintain the gains. Consider standard operating procedures, mistake proofing, visual management, total productive maintenance, and statistical process control (control charts). Work with the process owner to document the controls in a control plan.

A sample Control Plan is shown on the following pages. The numbers in the figure correspond to the numbers in the description below.

The administrative section of the control plan (sections 1-3) provides key identification, approval, and document control information. The main body of the control plan provides substantive information on the process, reactions to out-of-control conditions, and links to standard operating procedures.

1. The process information area should clearly and uniquely identify the process affected by the control plan

2. The process owners should approve of the plan

3. The document control section provides for identification, traceability, and retrieval of the control plan document itself. For a control plan to be effective, it must be a living document; therefore, the plan must contain space to document revision

---

4. The Process Step field identifies the scope of the process being controlled

5. The Variable field identifies the name of the characteristic being controlled

6. The CTS Type field indicates if the process step generates a KPIV (directly linked to a KPOV) or a KPOV (directly affecting the customer)

7. The Specification field provides a succinct description of what is being checked/evaluated and what are the criteria (e.g., specification limits)

8. The Control Method field identifies what type of control is being utilized (e.g., mistake proofing, control chart, etc.)

9. The Measurement System, Responsibility, Frequency, Sample Size, and Reporting fields define the actual evaluation details

10. The Out of Control Action Plan and the SOP Reference fields provide response instructions if the process were to show nonconformance as a result of the inspection/evaluation activities as documented in the previous fields. It should include process shutdown or quarantine authority/ procedures if appropriate, and show links to where other supporting documents, procedures, or policies (such as the organization's quality system) are documented

11. An optional Audit column (not shown on this form) can provide clear linkage to ISO or QS audit systems. These audits can be on the output of the process (y's), on the inputs of the process (x's), or can be designed to ensure that the project controls are still in place

Example DMAIC Project Control Plan

Control Plan

Process: On-site equipment repair | **Process Owner:** Bill Smith | **Revision/Approval:** Revision 1, approved by Kerry Jones

Process step	Variable	CTS variable type (input or output)	Specification	Control method	Measurement system	Responsibility	Sample frequency	Sample size and sub grouping	How is data reported?	Out of Control Action Plan	Standard Operating Procedures and References
Diagnose symptoms	Time to diagnose	Input	USL 15 min	SPC	Tablet time recorder (passed MSA Feb)	Zone supervisors	Weekly	All repairs within a week (typically 25-50)	Xbar-R chart	Supervisor investigates special cause, puts fix in place, and monitors	Doc S12.3
Document repair case	Completion rate	Input	100% completed	Mistake proofing (software does not allow case closure until documentation is complete)	NA	NA	NA		NA	Audit software annually	Doc S12.3
Completed repair	Total time to repair equipment	Output	USL 2.5 h	SPC	Tablet time recorder (passed MSA Feb)	Zone supervisors	Weekly	All repairs within a week (typically 25-50)	Xbar-R chart	Supervisor investigates special cause, puts fix in place, and monitors	Doc S12.3

What is being controlled — **1**; *Control chart information* — **2**; *Control actions* — **3**

Notes

Standard Z Table

Z	0	0.01	0.02	0.03	0.04	0.05	0.06	0.07	0.08	0.09
-4.0	0.00003	0.00003	0.00003	0.00003	0.00003	0.00003	0.00002	0.00002	0.00002	0.00002
-3.9	0.00005	0.00005	0.00004	0.00004	0.00004	0.00004	0.00004	0.00004	0.00003	0.00003
-3.8	0.00007	0.00007	0.00007	0.00006	0.00006	0.00006	0.00006	0.00005	0.00005	0.00005
-3.7	0.00011	0.00010	0.00010	0.00010	0.00009	0.00009	0.00008	0.00008	0.00008	0.00008
-3.6	0.00016	0.00015	0.00015	0.00014	0.00014	0.00013	0.00013	0.00012	0.00012	0.00011
-3.5	0.00023	0.00022	0.00022	0.00021	0.00020	0.00019	0.00019	0.00018	0.00017	0.00017
-3.4	0.00034	0.00032	0.00031	0.00030	0.00029	0.00028	0.00027	0.00026	0.00025	0.00024
-3.3	0.00048	0.00047	0.00045	0.00043	0.00042	0.00040	0.00039	0.00038	0.00036	0.00035
-3.2	0.00069	0.00066	0.00064	0.00062	0.00060	0.00058	0.00056	0.00054	0.00052	0.00050
-3.1	0.00097	0.00094	0.00090	0.00087	0.00084	0.00082	0.00079	0.00076	0.00074	0.00071
-3.0	0.00135	0.00131	0.00126	0.00122	0.00118	0.00114	0.00111	0.00107	0.00103	0.00100
-2.9	0.00187	0.00181	0.00175	0.00169	0.00164	0.00159	0.00154	0.00150	0.00144	0.00139
-2.8	0.00256	0.00248	0.00240	0.00233	0.00226	0.00219	0.00212	0.00205	0.00199	0.00193
-2.7	0.00347	0.00336	0.00326	0.00317	0.00307	0.00298	0.00289	0.00280	0.00272	0.00264
-2.6	0.00466	0.00453	0.00440	0.00427	0.00415	0.00402	0.00391	0.00379	0.00368	0.00357
-2.5	0.00621	0.00604	0.00587	0.00570	0.00554	0.00539	0.00523	0.00508	0.00494	0.00480
-2.4	0.00820	0.00798	0.00776	0.00755	0.00734	0.00714	0.00695	0.00676	0.00657	0.00639
-2.3	0.01072	0.01044	0.01017	0.00990	0.00964	0.00939	0.00914	0.00889	0.00866	0.00842
-2.2	0.01390	0.01355	0.01321	0.01287	0.01255	0.01222	0.01191	0.01160	0.01130	0.01101
-2.1	0.01786	0.01743	0.01700	0.01659	0.01618	0.01578	0.01539	0.01500	0.01463	0.01426
-2.0	0.02275	0.02222	0.02169	0.02118	0.02067	0.02018	0.01970	0.01923	0.01876	0.01831

Standard Z Table, continued

Z	0	0.01	0.02	0.03	0.04	0.05	0.06	0.07	0.08	0.09
-1.9	0.02872	0.02807	0.02743	0.02680	0.02619	0.02559	0.02500	0.02442	0.02385	0.02330
-1.8	0.03593	0.03515	0.03438	0.03362	0.03288	0.03216	0.03144	0.03074	0.03005	0.02938
-1.7	0.04456	0.04363	0.04272	0.04181	0.04093	0.04006	0.03920	0.03836	0.03754	0.03673
-1.6	0.05480	0.05370	0.05262	0.05155	0.05050	0.04947	0.04846	0.04746	0.04648	0.04551
-1.5	0.06681	0.06552	0.06425	0.06301	0.06178	0.06057	0.05938	0.05821	0.05705	0.05592
-1.4	0.08076	0.07927	0.07780	0.07636	0.07493	0.07353	0.07214	0.07078	0.06944	0.06811
-1.3	0.09680	0.09510	0.09342	0.09176	0.09012	0.08851	0.08691	0.08534	0.08379	0.08226
-1.2	0.11507	0.11314	0.11123	0.10935	0.10749	0.10565	0.10383	0.10204	0.10027	0.09852
-1.1	0.13566	0.13350	0.13136	0.12924	0.12714	0.12507	0.12302	0.12100	0.11900	0.11702
-1.0	0.15865	0.15625	0.15386	0.15150	0.14917	0.14686	0.14457	0.14231	0.14007	0.13786
-0.9	0.18406	0.18141	0.17878	0.17618	0.17361	0.17105	0.16853	0.16602	0.16354	0.16109
-0.8	0.21185	0.20897	0.20611	0.20327	0.20045	0.19766	0.19489	0.19215	0.18943	0.18673
-0.7	0.24196	0.23885	0.23576	0.23269	0.22965	0.22663	0.22363	0.22065	0.21769	0.21476
-0.6	0.27425	0.27093	0.26763	0.26434	0.26108	0.25784	0.25462	0.25143	0.24825	0.24509
-0.5	0.30853	0.30502	0.30153	0.29805	0.29460	0.29116	0.28774	0.28434	0.28095	0.27759
-0.4	0.34457	0.34090	0.33724	0.33360	0.32997	0.32635	0.32276	0.31917	0.31561	0.31206
-0.3	0.38209	0.37828	0.37448	0.37070	0.36692	0.36317	0.35942	0.35569	0.35197	0.34826
-0.2	0.42074	0.41683	0.41293	0.40904	0.40516	0.40129	0.39743	0.39358	0.38974	0.38590
-0.1	0.46017	0.45620	0.45224	0.44828	0.44433	0.44038	0.43644	0.43250	0.42857	0.42465
-0.0	0.50000	0.49601	0.49202	0.48803	0.48404	0.48006	0.47607	0.47209	0.46811	0.46414

Z to DPMO
Conversion Table

Sigma Level - Tenths	Sigma Level* - Hundredths									
	0.00	0.01	0.02	0.03	0.04	0.05	0.06	0.07	0.08	0.09
1.5	500,000	496,000	492,000	488,000	484,000	480,100	476,100	472,100	468,100	464,100
1.6	460,200	456,200	452,200	448,300	444,300	440,400	436,400	432,500	428,600	424,700
1.7	420,700	416,800	412,900	409,000	405,200	401,300	397,400	393,600	389,700	385,900
1.8	382,100	378,300	374,500	370,700	366,900	363,200	359,400	355,700	352,000	348,300
1.9	344,600	340,900	337,200	333,600	330,000	326,400	322,800	319,200	315,600	312,100
2.0	308,500	305,000	301,500	298,100	294,600	291,200	287,700	284,300	281,000	277,600
2.1	274,300	270,900	267,600	264,300	261,100	257,800	254,600	251,400	248,300	245,100
2.2	242,000	238,900	235,800	232,700	229,700	226,600	223,600	220,700	217,700	214,800
2.3	211,900	209,000	206,100	203,300	200,500	197,700	194,900	192,200	189,400	186,700
2.4	184,100	181,400	178,800	176,200	173,600	171,100	168,500	166,000	163,500	161,100
2.5	158,700	156,200	153,900	151,500	149,200	146,900	144,600	142,300	140,100	137,900
2.6	135,700	133,500	131,400	129,200	127,100	125,100	123,000	121,000	119,000	117,000
2.7	115,100	113,100	111,200	109,300	107,500	105,600	103,800	102,000	100,300	98,530
2.8	96,800	95,100	93,420	91,760	90,120	88,510	86,910	85,340	83,790	82,260
2.9	80,760	79,270	77,800	76,360	74,930	73,530	72,140	70,780	69,440	68,110
3.0	66,810	65,520	64,260	63,010	61,780	60,570	59,380	58,210	57,050	55,920
3.1	54,800	53,700	52,620	51,550	50,500	49,470	48,460	47,460	46,480	45,510
3.2	44,570	43,630	42,720	41,820	40,930	40,060	39,200	38,360	37,540	36,730
3.3	35,930	35,150	34,380	33,630	32,880	32,160	31,440	30,740	30,050	29,380
3.4	28,720	28,070	27,430	26,800	26,190	25,590	25,000	24,420	23,850	23,300
3.5	22,750	22,220	21,690	21,180	20,680	20,180	19,700	19,203	18,760	18,310
3.6	17,860	17,430	17,000	16,590	16,180	15,780	15,390	15,000	14,630	14,260
3.7	13,900	13,550	13,210	12,870	12,550	12,220	11,910	11,600	11,300	11,010
3.8	10,720	10,440	10,170	9,903	9,642	9,387	9,137	8,894	8,656	8,424
3.9	8,198	7,976	7,760	7,549	7,344	7,143	6,947	6,756	6,569	6,387
4.0	6,210	6,036	5,868	5,703	5,543	5,386	5,234	5,085	4,940	4,799

Z to DPMO
Conversion Table, continued

Sigma Level - Tenths	Sigma Level* - Hundredths									
	0.00	0.01	0.02	0.03	0.04	0.05	0.06	0.07	0.08	0.09
4.1	4,661	4,527	4,396	4,269	4,145	4,024	3,907	3,792	3,681	3,572
4.2	3,467	3,364	3,264	3,167	3,072	2,980	2,890	2,803	2,718	2,635
4.3	2,555	2,477	2,401	2,327	2,256	2,186	2,118	2,052	1,988	1,926
4.4	1,866	1,807	1,750	1,695	1,641	1,589	1,538	1,489	1,441	1,395
4.5	1,350	1,306	1,264	1,223	1,183	1,144	1,107	1,070	1,035	1,001
4.6	968	935	904	874	845	816	789	762	736	711
4.7	687	664	641	619	598	577	557	538	519	501
4.8	484	467	450	434	419	404	390	376	363	350
4.9	337	325	313	302	291	280	270	260	251	242
5.0	233	224	216	208	200	193	186	179	172	166
5.1	159	153	147	142	136	131	126	121	117	112
5.2	108	104	100	96	92	89	85	82	79	75
5.3	72	70	67	64	62	59	57	55	52	50
5.4	48	46	44	43	41	39	38	36	35	33
5.5	32	30	29	28	26	26	25	24	23	22
5.6	21.0	20.0	19.0	18.0	17.0	17.0	16.0	15.3	14.7	14.0
5.7	13.4	12.9	12.3	11.7	11.3	10.8	10.3	9.9	9.4	9.0
5.8	8.6	8.2	7.9	7.5	7.2	6.9	6.6	6.3	6.0	5.7
5.9	5.4	5.2	5.0	4.8	4.6	4.4	4.2	4.0	3.8	3.6
6.0	3.4	3.1	3.1	3.0	2.9	2.7	2.6	2.5	2.4	2.3

Example: 412,900 DPMO = 1.72 sigma, which, according to convention, is rounded-off to 1.7 sigma.
*1.5 sigma shift included.

Normal Distribution

z	0.00	0.01	0.02	0.03	0.04	0.05	0.06	0.07	0.08	0.09
0.0	0.5000	0.4960	0.4920	0.4880	0.4840	0.4801	0.4761	0.4721	0.4681	0.4641
0.1	0.4602	0.4562	0.4522	0.4483	0.4443	0.4404	0.4364	0.4325	0.4286	0.4247
0.2	0.4207	0.4168	0.4129	0.4090	0.4052	0.4013	0.3974	0.3936	0.3897	0.3859
0.3	0.3821	0.3783	0.3745	0.3707	0.3669	0.3632	0.3594	0.3557	0.3520	0.3483
0.4	0.3446	0.3409	0.3372	0.3336	0.3300	0.3264	0.3228	0.3192	0.3156	0.3121
0.5	0.3085	0.3050	0.3015	0.2981	0.2946	0.2912	0.2877	0.2843	0.2810	0.2776
0.6	0.2743	0.2709	0.2676	0.2643	0.2611	0.2578	0.2546	0.2514	0.2483	0.2451
0.7	0.2420	0.2389	0.2358	0.2327	0.2296	0.2266	0.2236	0.2206	0.2177	0.2148
0.8	0.2119	0.2090	0.2061	0.2033	0.2005	0.1977	0.1949	0.1922	0.1894	0.1867
0.9	0.1841	0.1814	0.1788	0.1762	0.1736	0.1711	0.1685	0.1660	0.1635	0.1611
1.0	0.1587	0.1562	0.1539	0.1515	0.1492	0.1469	0.1446	0.1423	0.1401	0.1379
1.1	0.1357	0.1335	0.1314	0.1292	0.1271	0.1251	0.1230	0.1210	0.1190	0.1170
1.2	0.1151	0.1131	0.1112	0.1093	0.1075	0.1056	0.1038	0.1020	0.1003	0.0985
1.3	0.0968	0.0951	0.0934	0.0918	0.0901	0.0885	0.0869	0.0853	0.0838	0.0823
1.4	0.0808	0.0793	0.0778	0.0764	0.0749	0.0735	0.0721	0.0708	0.0694	0.0681
1.5	0.0668	0.0655	0.0643	0.0630	0.0618	0.0606	0.0594	0.0582	0.0571	0.0559
1.6	0.0548	0.0537	0.0526	0.0516	0.0505	0.0495	0.0485	0.0475	0.0465	0.0455
1.7	0.0446	0.0436	0.0427	0.0418	0.0409	0.0401	0.0392	0.0384	0.0375	0.0367
1.8	0.0359	0.0351	0.0344	0.0336	0.0329	0.0322	0.0314	0.0307	0.0301	0.0294
1.9	0.0287	0.0281	0.0274	0.0268	0.0262	0.0256	0.0250	0.0244	0.0239	0.0233
2.0	0.0228	0.0222	0.0217	0.0212	0.0207	0.0202	0.0197	0.0192	0.0188	0.0183
2.1	0.0179	0.0174	0.0170	0.0166	0.0162	0.0158	0.0154	0.0150	0.0146	0.0143
2.2	0.0139	0.0136	0.0132	0.0129	0.0125	0.0122	0.0119	0.0116	0.0113	0.0110
2.3	0.0107	0.0104	0.0102	0.0099	0.0096	0.0094	0.0091	0.0089	0.0087	0.0084
2.4	0.0082	0.0080	0.0078	0.0075	0.0073	0.0071	0.0069	0.0068	0.0066	0.0064
2.5	0.0062	0.0060	0.0059	0.0057	0.0055	0.0054	0.0052	0.0051	0.0049	0.0048
2.6	0.0047	0.0045	0.0044	0.0043	0.0041	0.0040	0.0039	0.0038	0.0037	0.0036
2.7	0.0035	0.0034	0.0033	0.0032	0.0031	0.0030	0.0029	0.0028	0.0027	0.0026
2.8	0.0026	0.0025	0.0024	0.0023	0.0023	0.0022	0.0021	0.0021	0.0020	0.0019
2.9	0.0019	0.0018	0.0018	0.0017	0.0016	0.0016	0.0015	0.0015	0.0014	0.0014
3.0	0.0013	0.0013	0.0013	0.0012	0.0012	0.0011	0.0011	0.0011	0.0010	0.0010
3.1	0.0010	0.0009	0.0009	0.0009	0.0008	0.0008	0.0008	0.0008	0.0007	0.0007
3.2	0.0007	0.0007	0.0006	0.0006	0.0006	0.0006	0.0006	0.0005	0.0005	0.0005
3.3	0.0005	0.0005	0.0005	0.0004	0.0004	0.0004	0.0004	0.0004	0.0004	0.0003
3.4	0.0003	0.0003	0.0003	0.0003	0.0003	0.0003	0.0003	0.0003	0.0003	0.0002
3.5	0.0002	0.0002	0.0002	0.0002	0.0002	0.0002	0.0002	0.0002	0.0002	0.0002
3.6	0.0002	0.0002	0.0001	0.0001	0.0001	0.0001	0.0001	0.0001	0.0001	0.0001
3.7	0.0001	0.0001	0.0001	0.0001	0.0001	0.0001	0.0001	0.0001	0.0001	0.0001
3.8	0.0001	0.0001	0.0001	0.0001	0.0001	0.0001	0.0001	0.0001	0.0001	0.0001
3.9	0.0000	0.0000	0.0000	0.0000	0.0000	0.0000	0.0000	0.0000	0.0000	0.0000

Probability Points of t Distribution with v Degrees of Freedom

v	0.4	0.25	0.1	0.05	0.025	0.01	0.005	0.0025	0.001	0.0005
1	0.325	1.000	3.078	6.314	12.706	31.821	63.657	127.32	318.31	636.62
2	0.289	0.816	1.886	2.920	4.303	6.965	9.925	14.089	22.326	31.598
3	0.277	0.765	1.638	2.353	3.182	4.541	5.841	7.453	10.213	12.924
4	0.271	0.741	1.533	2.132	2.776	3.747	4.604	5.598	7.173	8.610
5	0.267	0.727	1.476	2.015	2.571	3.365	4.032	4.773	5.893	6.869
6	0.265	0.718	1.440	1.943	2.447	3.143	3.707	4.317	5.208	5.959
7	0.263	0.711	1.415	1.895	2.365	2.998	3.499	4.029	4.785	5.408
8	0.262	0.706	1.397	1.860	2.306	2.896	3.355	3.833	4.501	5.041
9	0.261	0.703	1.383	1.833	2.262	2.821	3.250	3.690	4.297	4.781
10	0.260	0.700	1.372	1.812	2.228	2.764	3.169	3.581	4.144	4.587
11	0.260	0.697	1.363	1.796	2.201	2.718	3.106	3.497	4.025	4.437
12	0.259	0.695	1.356	1.782	2.179	2.681	3.055	3.428	3.930	4.318
13	0.259	0.694	1.350	1.771	2.160	2.650	3.012	3.372	3.852	4.221
14	0.258	0.692	1.345	1.761	2.145	2.624	2.977	3.326	3.787	4.140
15	0.258	0.691	1.341	1.753	2.131	2.602	2.947	3.286	3.733	4.073
16	0.258	0.690	1.337	1.746	2.120	2.583	2.921	3.252	3.686	4.015
17	0.257	0.689	1.333	1.740	2.110	2.567	2.898	3.222	3.646	3.965
18	0.257	0.688	1.330	1.734	2.101	2.552	2.878	3.197	3.610	3.922
19	0.257	0.688	1.328	1.729	2.093	2.539	2.861	3.174	3.579	3.883
20	0.257	0.687	1.325	1.725	2.086	2.528	2.845	3.153	3.552	3.850
21	0.257	0.686	1.323	1.721	2.080	2.518	2.831	3.135	3.527	3.819
22	0.256	0.686	1.321	1.717	2.074	2.508	2.819	3.119	3.505	3.792
23	0.256	0.685	1.319	1.714	2.069	2.500	2.807	3.104	3.485	3.767
24	0.256	0.685	1.318	1.711	2.064	2.492	2.797	3.091	3.467	3.745
25	0.256	0.684	1.316	1.708	2.060	2.485	2.787	3.078	3.450	3.725
26	0.256	0.684	1.315	1.706	2.056	2.479	2.779	3.067	3.435	3.707
27	0.256	0.684	1.314	1.703	2.052	2.473	2.771	3.057	3.421	3.690
28	0.256	0.683	1.313	1.701	2.048	2.467	2.763	3.047	3.408	3.674
29	0.256	0.683	1.311	1.699	2.045	2.462	2.756	3.038	3.396	3.659
30	0.256	0.683	1.310	1.697	2.042	2.457	2.750	3.030	3.385	3.646
40	0.255	0.681	1.303	1.684	2.021	2.423	2.704	2.971	3.307	3.551
60	0.254	0.679	1.296	1.671	2.000	2.390	2.660	2.915	3.232	3.460
120	0.254	0.677	1.289	1.658	1.980	2.358	2.617	2.860	3.160	3.373
∞	0.253	0.674	1.282	1.645	1.960	2.326	2.576	2.807	3.090	3.291

Ordinates of t Distribution
v Degrees of Freedom

ordinate

v	0.00	0.25	0.50	0.75	1.00	1.25	1.50	1.75	2.00	2.25	2.50	2.75	3.00
1	0.318	0.300	0.255	0.204	0.159	0.124	0.098	0.078	0.064	0.053	0.044	0.037	0.032
2	0.354	0.338	0.296	0.244	0.193	0.149	0.114	0.088	0.068	0.053	0.042	0.034	0.027
3	0.368	0.353	0.313	0.261	0.207	0.159	0.120	0.090	0.068	0.051	0.039	0.030	0.023
4	0.375	0.361	0.322	0.270	0.215	0.164	0.123	0.091	0.066	0.049	0.036	0.026	0.020
5	0.380	0.366	0.328	0.276	0.220	0.168	0.125	0.091	0.065	0.047	0.033	0.024	0.017
6	0.383	0.369	0.332	0.280	0.223	0.170	0.126	0.090	0.064	0.045	0.032	0.022	0.016
7	0.385	0.372	0.335	0.283	0.226	0.172	0.126	0.090	0.063	0.044	0.030	0.021	0.014
8	0.387	0.373	0.337	0.285	0.228	0.173	0.127	0.090	0.062	0.043	0.029	0.019	0.013
9	0.388	0.375	0.338	0.287	0.229	0.174	0.127	0.090	0.062	0.042	0.028	0.018	0.012
10	0.389	0.376	0.340	0.288	0.230	0.175	0.127	0.090	0.061	0.041	0.027	0.018	0.011
11	0.390	0.377	0.341	0.289	0.231	0.176	0.128	0.089	0.061	0.040	0.026	0.017	0.011
12	0.391	0.378	0.342	0.290	0.232	0.176	0.128	0.089	0.060	0.040	0.026	0.016	0.010
13	0.391	0.378	0.343	0.291	0.233	0.177	0.128	0.089	0.060	0.039	0.025	0.016	0.010
14	0.392	0.379	0.343	0.292	0.234	0.177	0.128	0.089	0.060	0.039	0.025	0.015	0.010
15	0.392	0.380	0.344	0.292	0.234	0.177	0.128	0.089	0.059	0.038	0.024	0.015	0.009

Ordinates of t Distribution
v Degrees of Freedom,
continued

ordinate

v	0.00	0.25	0.50	0.75	1.00	1.25	1.50	1.75	2.00	2.25	2.50	2.75	3.00
16	0.393	0.380	0.344	0.293	0.235	0.178	0.128	0.089	0.059	0.038	0.024	0.015	0.009
17	0.393	0.380	0.345	0.293	0.235	0.178	0.128	0.089	0.059	0.038	0.024	0.014	0.009
18	0.393	0.381	0.345	0.294	0.235	0.178	0.129	0.088	0.059	0.037	0.023	0.014	0.008
19	0.394	0.381	0.346	0.294	0.236	0.179	0.129	0.088	0.058	0.037	0.023	0.014	0.008
20	0.394	0.381	0.346	0.294	0.236	0.179	0.129	0.088	0.058	0.037	0.023	0.014	0.008
22	0.394	0.382	0.346	0.295	0.237	0.179	0.129	0.088	0.058	0.036	0.022	0.013	0.008
24	0.395	0.382	0.347	0.296	0.237	0.179	0.129	0.088	0.057	0.036	0.022	0.013	0.007
26	0.395	0.383	0.347	0.296	0.237	0.180	0.129	0.088	0.057	0.036	0.022	0.013	0.007
28	0.395	0.383	0.348	0.296	0.238	0.180	0.129	0.088	0.057	0.036	0.021	0.012	0.007
30	0.396	0.383	0.348	0.297	0.238	0.180	0.129	0.088	0.057	0.035	0.021	0.012	0.007
35	0.396	0.384	0.348	0.297	0.239	0.180	0.129	0.088	0.056	0.035	0.021	0.012	0.006
40	0.396	0.384	0.349	0.298	0.239	0.181	0.129	0.087	0.056	0.035	0.020	0.011	0.006
45	0.397	0.384	0.349	0.298	0.239	0.181	0.129	0.087	0.056	0.034	0.020	0.011	0.006
50	0.397	0.385	0.350	0.298	0.240	0.181	0.129	0.087	0.056	0.034	0.020	0.011	0.006
8	0.399	0.387	0.352	0.301	0.242	0.183	0.130	0.086	0.054	0.032	0.018	0.009	0.004

χ² Distribution with v Degrees of Freedom

v	0.995	0.99	0.975	0.95	0.9	0.75	0.5	0.25	0.1	0.05	0.025	0.01	0.005	0.001
1	-	-	-	-	0.016	0.102	0.455	1.32	2.71	3.84	5.02	6.63	7.88	10.8
2	0.010	0.020	0.051	0.103	0.211	0.575	1.39	2.77	4.61	5.99	7.38	9.21	10.6	13.8
3	0.072	0.115	0.216	0.352	0.584	1.21	2.37	4.11	6.25	7.81	9.35	11.3	12.8	16.3
4	0.207	0.297	0.484	0.711	1.06	1.92	3.36	5.39	7.78	9.49	11.1	13.3	14.9	18.5
5	0.412	0.554	0.831	1.15	1.61	2.67	4.35	6.63	9.24	11.1	12.8	15.1	16.7	20.5
6	0.676	0.872	1.24	1.64	2.20	3.45	5.35	7.84	10.6	12.6	14.4	16.8	18.5	22.5
7	0.989	1.24	1.69	2.17	2.83	4.25	6.35	9.04	12.0	14.1	16.0	18.5	20.3	24.3
8	1.34	1.65	2.18	2.73	3.49	5.07	7.34	10.2	13.4	15.5	17.5	20.1	22.0	26.1
9	1.73	2.09	2.70	3.33	4.17	5.90	8.34	11.4	14.7	16.9	19.0	21.7	23.6	27.9
10	2.16	2.56	3.25	3.94	4.87	6.74	9.34	12.5	16.0	18.3	20.5	23.2	25.2	29.6
11	2.60	3.05	3.82	4.57	5.58	7.58	10.3	13.7	17.3	19.7	21.9	24.7	26.8	31.3
12	3.07	3.57	4.40	5.23	6.30	8.44	11.3	14.8	18.5	21.0	23.3	26.2	28.3	32.9
13	3.57	4.11	5.01	5.89	7.04	9.30	12.3	16.0	19.8	22.4	24.7	27.7	29.8	34.5
14	4.07	4.66	5.63	6.57	7.79	10.2	13.3	17.1	21.1	23.7	26.1	29.1	31.3	36.1
15	4.60	5.23	6.26	7.26	8.55	11.0	14.3	18.2	22.3	25.0	27.5	30.6	32.8	37.7

χ^2 Distribution with v Degrees of Freedom, continued

v	0.995	0.99	0.975	0.95	0.9	0.75	0.5	0.25	0.1	0.05	0.025	0.01	0.005	0.001
16	5.14	5.81	6.91	7.96	9.31	11.9	15.3	19.4	23.5	26.3	28.8	32.0	34.3	39.3
17	5.70	6.41	7.56	8.67	10.1	12.8	16.3	20.5	24.8	27.6	30.2	33.4	35.7	40.8
18	6.26	7.01	8.23	9.39	10.9	13.7	17.3	21.6	26.0	28.9	31.5	34.8	37.2	42.3
19	6.84	7.63	8.91	10.1	11.7	14.6	18.3	22.7	27.2	30.1	32.9	36.2	38.6	43.8
20	7.43	8.26	9.59	10.9	12.4	15.5	19.3	23.8	28.4	31.4	34.2	37.6	40.0	45.3
21	8.03	8.90	10.3	11.6	13.2	16.3	20.3	24.9	29.6	32.7	35.5	38.9	41.4	46.8
22	8.64	9.54	11.0	12.3	14.0	17.2	21.3	26.0	30.8	33.9	36.8	40.3	42.8	48.3
23	9.26	10.2	11.7	13.1	14.8	18.1	22.3	27.1	32.0	35.2	38.1	41.6	44.2	49.7
24	9.89	10.9	12.4	13.8	15.7	19.0	23.3	28.2	33.2	36.4	39.4	43.0	45.6	51.2
25	10.5	11.5	13.1	14.6	16.5	19.9	24.3	29.3	34.4	37.7	40.6	44.3	46.9	52.6
26	11.2	12.2	13.8	15.4	17.3	20.8	25.3	30.4	35.6	38.9	41.9	45.6	48.3	54.1
27	11.8	12.9	14.6	16.2	18.1	21.7	26.3	31.5	36.7	40.1	43.2	47.0	49.6	55.5
28	12.5	13.6	15.3	16.9	18.9	22.7	27.3	32.6	37.9	41.3	44.5	48.3	51.0	56.9
29	13.1	14.3	16.0	17.7	19.8	23.6	28.3	33.7	39.1	42.6	45.7	49.6	52.3	58.3
30	13.8	15.0	16.8	18.5	20.6	24.5	29.3	34.8	40.3	43.8	47.0	50.9	53.7	59.7

F distribution:
Upper 25% Points

v_2 \ v_1	1	2	3	4	5	6	7	8	9
1	5.83	7.50	8.20	8.58	8.82	8.98	9.10	9.19	9.26
2	2.57	3.00	3.15	3.23	3.28	3.31	3.34	3.35	3.37
3	2.02	2.28	2.36	2.39	2.41	2.42	2.43	2.44	2.44
4	1.81	2.00	2.05	2.06	2.07	2.08	2.08	2.08	2.08
5	1.69	1.85	1.88	1.89	1.89	1.89	1.89	1.89	1.89
6	1.62	1.76	1.78	1.79	1.79	1.78	1.78	1.78	1.77
7	1.57	1.70	1.72	1.72	1.71	1.71	1.70	1.70	1.69
8	1.54	1.66	1.67	1.66	1.66	1.65	1.64	1.64	1.63
9	1.51	1.62	1.63	1.63	1.62	1.61	1.60	1.60	1.59
10	1.49	1.60	1.60	1.59	1.59	1.58	1.57	1.56	1.56
11	1.47	1.58	1.58	1.57	1.56	1.55	1.54	1.53	1.53
12	1.46	1.56	1.56	1.55	1.54	1.53	1.52	1.51	1.51
13	1.45	1.55	1.55	1.53	1.52	1.51	1.50	1.49	1.49
14	1.44	1.53	1.53	1.52	1.51	1.50	1.49	1.48	1.47
15	1.43	1.52	1.52	1.51	1.49	1.48	1.47	1.46	1.46
16	1.42	1.51	1.51	1.50	1.48	1.47	1.46	1.45	1.44
17	1.42	1.51	1.50	1.49	1.47	1.46	1.45	1.44	1.43
18	1.41	1.50	1.49	1.48	1.46	1.45	1.44	1.43	1.42
19	1.41	1.49	1.49	1.47	1.46	1.44	1.43	1.42	1.41
20	1.40	1.49	1.48	1.47	1.45	1.44	1.43	1.42	1.41
21	1.40	1.48	1.48	1.46	1.44	1.43	1.42	1.41	1.40
22	1.40	1.48	1.47	1.45	1.44	1.42	1.41	1.40	1.39
23	1.39	1.47	1.47	1.45	1.43	1.42	1.41	1.40	1.39
24	1.39	1.47	1.46	1.44	1.43	1.41	1.40	1.39	1.38
25	1.39	1.47	1.46	1.44	1.42	1.41	1.40	1.39	1.38
26	1.38	1.46	1.45	1.44	1.42	1.41	1.39	1.38	1.37
27	1.38	1.46	1.45	1.43	1.42	1.40	1.39	1.38	1.37
28	1.38	1.46	1.45	1.43	1.41	1.40	1.39	1.38	1.37
29	1.38	1.45	1.45	1.43	1.41	1.40	1.38	1.37	1.36
30	1.38	1.45	1.44	1.42	1.41	1.39	1.38	1.37	1.36
40	1.36	1.44	1.42	1.40	1.39	1.37	1.36	1.35	1.34
60	1.35	1.42	1.41	1.38	1.37	1.35	1.33	1.32	1.31
120	1.34	1.40	1.39	1.37	1.35	1.33	1.31	1.30	1.29
∞	1.32	1.39	1.37	1.35	1.33	1.31	1.29	1.28	1.27

F distribution:
Upper 25% Points, continued

v_2 \ v_1	10	12	15	20	24	30	40	60	120	∞
1	9.32	9.41	9.49	9.58	9.63	9.67	9.71	9.76	9.80	9.85
2	3.38	3.39	3.41	3.43	3.43	3.44	3.45	3.46	3.47	3.48
3	2.44	2.45	2.46	2.46	2.46	2.47	2.47	2.47	2.47	2.47
4	2.08	2.08	2.08	2.08	2.08	2.08	2.08	2.08	2.08	2.08
5	1.89	1.89	1.89	1.88	1.88	1.88	1.88	1.87	1.87	1.87
6	1.77	1.77	1.76	1.76	1.75	1.75	1.75	1.74	1.74	1.74
7	1.69	1.68	1.68	1.67	1.67	1.66	1.66	1.65	1.65	1.65
8	1.63	1.62	1.62	1.61	1.60	1.60	1.59	1.59	1.58	1.58
9	1.59	1.58	1.57	1.56	1.56	1.55	1.54	1.54	1.53	1.53
10	1.55	1.54	1.53	1.52	1.52	1.51	1.51	1.50	1.49	1.48
11	1.52	1.51	1.50	1.49	1.49	1.48	1.47	1.47	1.46	1.45
12	1.50	1.49	1.48	1.47	1.46	1.45	1.45	1.44	1.43	1.42
13	1.48	1.47	1.46	1.45	1.44	1.43	1.42	1.42	1.41	1.40
14	1.46	1.45	1.44	1.43	1.42	1.41	1.41	1.40	1.39	1.38
15	1.45	1.44	1.43	1.41	1.41	1.40	1.39	1.38	1.37	1.36
16	1.44	1.43	1.41	1.40	1.39	1.38	1.37	1.36	1.35	1.34
17	1.43	1.41	1.40	1.39	1.38	1.37	1.36	1.35	1.34	1.33
18	1.42	1.40	1.39	1.38	1.37	1.36	1.35	1.34	1.33	1.32
19	1.41	1.40	1.38	1.37	1.36	1.35	1.34	1.33	1.32	1.30
20	1.40	1.39	1.37	1.36	1.35	1.34	1.33	1.32	1.31	1.29
21	1.39	1.38	1.37	1.35	1.34	1.33	1.32	1.31	1.30	1.28
22	1.39	1.37	1.36	1.34	1.33	1.32	1.31	1.30	1.29	1.28
23	1.38	1.37	1.35	1.34	1.33	1.32	1.31	1.30	1.28	1.27
24	1.38	1.36	1.35	1.33	1.32	1.31	1.30	1.29	1.28	1.26
25	1.37	1.36	1.34	1.33	1.32	1.31	1.29	1.28	1.27	1.25
26	1.37	1.35	1.34	1.32	1.31	1.30	1.29	1.28	1.26	1.25
27	1.36	1.35	1.33	1.32	1.31	1.30	1.28	1.27	1.26	1.24
28	1.36	1.34	1.33	1.31	1.30	1.29	1.28	1.27	1.25	1.24
29	1.35	1.34	1.32	1.31	1.30	1.29	1.27	1.26	1.25	1.23
30	1.35	1.34	1.32	1.30	1.29	1.28	1.27	1.26	1.24	1.23
40	1.33	1.31	1.30	1.28	1.26	1.25	1.24	1.22	1.21	1.19
60	1.30	1.29	1.27	1.25	1.24	1.22	1.21	1.19	1.17	1.15
120	1.28	1.26	1.24	1.22	1.21	1.19	1.18	1.16	1.13	1.10
∞	1.25	1.24	1.22	1.19	1.18	1.16	1.14	1.12	1.08	1.00

F distribution:
Upper 10% Points

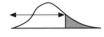

v_2 \ v_1	1	2	3	4	5	6	7	8	9
1	39.86	49.50	53.59	55.83	57.24	58.20	58.91	59.44	59.86
2	8.53	9.00	9.16	9.24	9.29	9.33	9.35	9.37	9.38
3	5.54	5.46	5.39	5.34	5.31	5.28	5.27	5.25	5.24
4	4.54	4.32	4.19	4.11	4.05	4.01	3.98	3.95	3.94
5	4.06	3.78	3.62	3.52	3.45	3.40	3.37	3.34	3.32
6	3.78	3.46	3.29	3.18	3.11	3.05	3.01	2.98	2.96
7	3.59	3.26	3.07	2.96	2.88	2.83	2.78	2.75	2.72
8	3.46	3.11	2.92	2.81	2.73	2.67	2.62	2.59	2.56
9	3.36	3.01	2.81	2.69	2.61	2.55	2.51	2.47	2.44
10	3.29	2.92	2.73	2.61	2.52	2.46	2.41	2.38	2.35
11	3.23	2.86	2.66	2.54	2.45	2.39	2.34	2.30	2.27
12	3.18	2.81	2.61	2.48	2.39	2.33	2.28	2.24	2.21
13	3.14	2.76	2.56	2.43	2.35	2.28	2.23	2.20	2.16
14	3.10	2.73	2.52	2.39	2.31	2.24	2.19	2.15	2.12
15	3.07	2.70	2.49	2.36	2.27	2.21	2.16	2.12	2.09
16	3.05	2.67	2.46	2.33	2.24	2.18	2.13	2.09	2.06
17	3.03	2.64	2.44	2.31	2.22	2.15	2.10	2.06	2.03
18	3.01	2.62	2.42	2.29	2.20	2.13	2.08	2.04	2.00
19	2.99	2.61	2.40	2.27	2.18	2.11	2.06	2.02	1.98
20	2.97	2.59	2.38	2.25	2.16	2.09	2.04	2.00	1.96
21	2.96	2.57	2.36	2.23	2.14	2.08	2.02	1.98	1.95
22	2.95	2.56	2.35	2.22	2.13	2.06	2.01	1.97	1.93
23	2.94	2.55	2.34	2.21	2.11	2.05	1.99	1.95	1.92
24	2.93	2.54	2.33	2.19	2.10	2.04	1.98	1.94	1.91
25	2.92	2.53	2.32	2.18	2.09	2.02	1.97	1.93	1.89
26	2.91	2.52	2.31	2.17	2.08	2.01	1.96	1.92	1.88
27	2.90	2.51	2.30	2.17	2.07	2.00	1.95	1.91	1.87
28	2.89	2.50	2.29	2.16	2.06	2.00	1.94	1.90	1.87
29	2.89	2.50	2.28	2.15	2.06	1.99	1.93	1.89	1.86
30	2.88	2.49	2.28	2.14	2.05	1.98	1.93	1.88	1.85
40	2.84	2.44	2.23	2.09	2.00	1.93	1.87	1.83	1.79
60	2.79	2.39	2.18	2.04	1.95	1.87	1.82	1.77	1.74
120	2.75	2.35	2.13	1.99	1.90	1.82	1.77	1.72	1.68
∞	2.71	2.30	2.08	1.94	1.85	1.77	1.72	1.67	1.63

v_2 \ v_1	10	12	15	20	24	30	40	60	120	∞
1	60.19	60.71	61.22	61.74	62.00	62.26	62.53	62.79	63.06	63.33
2	9.39	9.41	9.42	9.44	9.45	9.46	9.47	9.47	9.48	9.49
3	5.23	5.22	5.20	5.18	5.18	5.17	5.16	5.15	5.14	5.13
4	3.92	3.90	3.87	3.84	3.83	3.82	3.80	3.79	3.78	3.76
5	3.30	3.27	3.24	3.21	3.19	3.17	3.16	3.14	3.12	3.10
6	2.94	2.90	2.87	2.84	2.82	2.80	2.78	2.76	2.74	2.72
7	2.70	2.67	2.63	2.59	2.58	2.56	2.54	2.51	2.49	2.47
8	2.54	2.50	2.46	2.42	2.40	2.38	2.36	2.34	2.32	2.29
9	2.42	2.38	2.34	2.30	2.28	2.25	2.23	2.21	2.18	2.16
10	2.32	2.28	2.24	2.20	2.18	2.16	2.13	2.11	2.08	2.06
11	2.25	2.21	2.17	2.12	2.10	2.08	2.05	2.03	2.00	1.97
12	2.19	2.15	2.10	2.06	2.04	2.01	1.99	1.96	1.93	1.90
13	2.14	2.10	2.05	2.01	1.98	1.96	1.93	1.90	1.88	1.85
14	2.10	2.05	2.01	1.96	1.94	1.91	1.89	1.86	1.83	1.80
15	2.06	2.02	1.97	1.92	1.90	1.87	1.85	1.82	1.79	1.76
16	2.03	1.99	1.94	1.89	1.87	1.84	1.81	1.78	1.75	1.72
17	2.00	1.96	1.91	1.86	1.84	1.81	1.78	1.75	1.72	1.69
18	1.98	1.93	1.89	1.84	1.81	1.78	1.75	1.72	1.69	1.66
19	1.96	1.91	1.86	1.81	1.79	1.76	1.73	1.70	1.67	1.63
20	1.94	1.89	1.84	1.79	1.77	1.74	1.71	1.68	1.64	1.61
21	1.92	1.87	1.83	1.78	1.75	1.72	1.69	1.66	1.62	1.59
22	1.90	1.86	1.81	1.76	1.73	1.70	1.67	1.64	1.60	1.57
23	1.89	1.84	1.80	1.74	1.72	1.69	1.66	1.62	1.59	1.55
24	1.88	1.83	1.78	1.73	1.70	1.67	1.64	1.61	1.57	1.53
25	1.87	1.82	1.77	1.72	1.69	1.66	1.63	1.59	1.56	1.52
26	1.86	1.81	1.76	1.71	1.68	1.65	1.61	1.58	1.54	1.50
27	1.85	1.80	1.75	1.70	1.67	1.64	1.60	1.57	1.53	1.49
28	1.84	1.79	1.74	1.69	1.66	1.63	1.59	1.56	1.52	1.48
29	1.83	1.78	1.73	1.68	1.65	1.62	1.58	1.55	1.51	1.47
30	1.82	1.77	1.72	1.67	1.64	1.61	1.57	1.54	1.50	1.46
40	1.76	1.71	1.66	1.61	1.57	1.54	1.51	1.47	1.42	1.38
60	1.71	1.66	1.60	1.54	1.51	1.48	1.44	1.40	1.35	1.29
120	1.65	1.60	1.55	1.48	1.45	1.41	1.37	1.32	1.26	1.19
∞	1.60	1.55	1.49	1.42	1.38	1.34	1.30	1.24	1.17	1.00

v_2 \ v_1	1	2	3	4	5	6	7	8	9
1	161.4	199.5	215.7	224.6	230.2	234.0	236.8	238.9	240.5
2	18.51	19.00	19.16	19.25	19.30	19.33	19.35	19.37	19.38
3	10.13	9.55	9.28	9.12	9.01	8.94	8.89	8.85	8.81
4	7.71	6.94	6.59	6.39	6.26	6.16	6.09	6.04	6.00
5	6.61	5.79	5.41	5.19	5.05	4.95	4.88	4.82	4.77
6	5.99	5.14	4.76	4.53	4.39	4.28	4.21	4.15	4.10
7	5.59	4.74	4.35	4.12	3.97	3.87	3.79	3.73	3.68
8	5.32	4.46	4.07	3.84	3.69	3.58	3.50	3.44	3.39
9	5.12	4.26	3.86	3.63	3.48	3.37	3.29	3.23	3.18
10	4.96	4.10	3.71	3.48	3.33	3.22	3.14	3.07	3.02
11	4.84	3.98	3.59	3.36	3.20	3.09	3.01	2.95	2.90
12	4.75	3.89	3.49	3.26	3.11	3.00	2.91	2.85	2.80
13	4.67	3.81	3.41	3.18	3.03	2.92	2.83	2.77	2.71
14	4.60	3.74	3.34	3.11	2.96	2.85	2.76	2.70	2.65
15	4.54	3.68	3.29	3.06	2.90	2.79	2.71	2.64	2.59
16	4.49	3.63	3.24	3.01	2.85	2.74	2.66	2.59	2.54
17	4.45	3.59	3.20	2.96	2.81	2.70	2.61	2.55	2.49
18	4.41	3.55	3.16	2.93	2.77	2.66	2.58	2.51	2.46
19	4.38	3.52	3.13	2.90	2.74	2.63	2.54	2.48	2.42
20	4.35	3.49	3.10	2.87	2.71	2.60	2.51	2.45	2.39
21	4.32	3.47	3.07	2.84	2.68	2.57	2.49	2.42	2.37
22	4.30	3.44	3.05	2.82	2.66	2.55	2.46	2.40	2.34
23	4.28	3.42	3.03	2.80	2.64	2.53	2.44	2.37	2.32
24	4.26	3.40	3.01	2.78	2.62	2.51	2.42	2.36	2.30
25	4.24	3.39	2.99	2.76	2.60	2.49	2.40	2.34	2.28
26	4.23	3.37	2.98	2.74	2.59	2.47	2.39	2.32	2.27
27	4.21	3.35	2.96	2.73	2.57	2.46	2.37	2.31	2.25
28	4.20	3.34	2.95	2.71	2.56	2.45	2.36	2.29	2.24
29	4.18	3.33	2.93	2.70	2.55	2.43	2.35	2.28	2.22
30	4.17	3.32	2.92	2.69	2.53	2.42	2.33	2.27	2.21
40	4.08	3.23	2.84	2.61	2.45	2.34	2.25	2.18	2.12
60	4.00	3.15	2.76	2.53	2.37	2.25	2.17	2.10	2.04
120	3.92	3.07	2.68	2.45	2.29	2.17	2.09	2.02	1.96
∞	3.84	3.00	2.60	2.37	2.21	2.10	2.01	1.94	1.88

v_1 v_2	10	12	15	20	24	30	40	60	120	∞
1	241.9	243.9	245.9	248.0	249.1	250.1	251.1	252.2	253.3	254.3
2	19.40	19.41	19.43	19.45	19.45	19.46	19.47	19.48	19.49	19.50
3	8.79	8.74	8.70	8.66	8.64	8.62	8.59	8.57	8.55	8.53
4	5.96	5.91	5.86	5.80	5.77	5.75	5.72	5.69	5.66	5.63
5	4.74	4.68	4.62	4.56	4.53	4.50	4.46	4.43	4.40	4.36
6	4.06	4.00	3.94	3.87	3.84	3.81	3.77	3.74	3.70	3.67
7	3.64	3.57	3.51	3.44	3.41	3.38	3.34	3.30	3.27	3.23
8	3.35	3.28	3.22	3.15	3.12	3.08	3.04	3.01	2.97	2.93
9	3.14	3.07	3.01	2.94	2.90	2.86	2.83	2.79	2.75	2.71
10	2.98	2.91	2.85	2.77	2.74	2.70	2.66	2.62	2.58	2.54
11	2.85	2.79	2.72	2.65	2.61	2.57	2.53	2.49	2.45	2.40
12	2.75	2.69	2.62	2.54	2.51	2.47	2.43	2.38	2.34	2.30
13	2.67	2.60	2.53	2.46	2.42	2.38	2.34	2.30	2.25	2.21
14	2.60	2.53	2.46	2.39	2.35	2.31	2.27	2.22	2.18	2.13
15	2.54	2.48	2.40	2.33	2.29	2.25	2.20	2.16	2.11	2.07
16	2.49	2.42	2.35	2.28	2.24	2.19	2.15	2.11	2.06	2.01
17	2.45	2.38	2.31	2.23	2.19	2.15	2.10	2.06	2.01	1.96
18	2.41	2.34	2.27	2.19	2.15	2.11	2.06	2.02	1.97	1.92
19	2.38	2.31	2.23	2.16	2.11	2.07	2.03	1.98	1.93	1.88
20	2.35	2.28	2.20	2.12	2.08	2.04	1.99	1.95	1.90	1.84
21	2.32	2.25	2.18	2.10	2.05	2.01	1.96	1.92	1.87	1.81
22	2.30	2.23	2.15	2.07	2.03	1.98	1.94	1.89	1.84	1.78
23	2.27	2.20	2.13	2.05	2.01	1.96	1.91	1.86	1.81	1.76
24	2.25	2.18	2.11	2.03	1.98	1.94	1.89	1.84	1.79	1.73
25	2.24	2.16	2.09	2.01	1.96	1.92	1.87	1.82	1.77	1.71
26	2.22	2.15	2.07	1.99	1.95	1.90	1.85	1.80	1.75	1.69
27	2.20	2.13	2.06	1.97	1.93	1.88	1.84	1.79	1.73	1.67
28	2.19	2.12	2.04	1.96	1.91	1.87	1.82	1.77	1.71	1.65
29	2.18	2.10	2.03	1.94	1.90	1.85	1.81	1.75	1.70	1.64
30	2.16	2.09	2.01	1.93	1.89	1.84	1.79	1.74	1.68	1.62
40	2.08	2.00	1.92	1.84	1.79	1.74	1.69	1.64	1.58	1.51
60	1.99	1.92	1.84	1.75	1.70	1.65	1.59	1.53	1.47	1.39
120	1.91	1.83	1.75	1.66	1.61	1.55	1.50	1.43	1.35	1.25
∞	1.83	1.75	1.67	1.57	1.52	1.46	1.39	1.32	1.22	1.00

F distribution:
Upper 1% Points

v_2 \ v_1	1	2	3	4	5	6	7	8	9
1	4052	4999.50	5403	5625	5764	5859	5928	5982	6022
2	98.50	99.00	99.17	99.25	99.30	99.33	99.36	99.37	99.39
3	34.12	30.82	29.46	28.71	28.24	27.91	27.67	27.49	27.35
4	21.20	18.00	16.69	15.98	15.52	15.21	14.98	14.80	14.66
5	16.26	13.27	12.06	11.39	10.97	10.67	10.46	10.29	10.16
6	13.75	10.92	9.78	9.15	8.75	8.47	8.26	8.10	7.98
7	12.25	9.55	8.45	7.85	7.46	7.19	6.99	6.84	6.72
8	11.26	8.65	7.59	7.01	6.63	6.37	6.18	6.03	5.91
9	10.56	8.02	6.99	6.42	6.06	5.80	5.61	5.47	5.35
10	10.04	7.56	6.55	5.99	5.64	5.39	5.20	5.06	4.94
11	9.65	7.21	6.22	5.67	5.32	5.07	4.89	4.74	4.63
12	9.33	6.93	5.95	5.41	5.06	4.82	4.64	4.50	4.39
13	9.07	6.70	5.74	5.21	4.86	4.62	4.44	4.30	4.19
14	8.86	6.51	5.56	5.04	4.69	4.46	4.28	4.14	4.03
15	8.68	6.36	5.42	4.89	4.56	4.32	4.14	4.00	3.89
16	8.53	6.23	5.29	4.77	4.44	4.20	4.03	3.89	3.78
17	8.40	6.11	5.18	4.67	4.34	4.10	3.93	3.79	3.68
18	8.29	6.01	5.09	4.58	4.25	4.01	3.84	3.71	3.60
19	8.18	5.93	5.01	4.50	4.17	3.94	3.77	3.63	3.52
20	8.10	5.85	4.94	4.43	4.10	3.87	3.70	3.56	3.46
21	8.02	5.78	4.87	4.37	4.04	3.81	3.64	3.51	3.40
22	7.95	5.72	4.82	4.31	3.99	3.76	3.59	3.45	3.35
23	7.88	5.66	4.76	4.26	3.94	3.71	3.54	3.41	3.30
24	7.82	5.61	4.72	4.22	3.90	3.67	3.50	3.36	3.26
25	7.77	5.57	4.68	4.18	3.85	3.63	3.46	3.32	3.22
26	7.72	5.53	4.64	4.14	3.82	3.59	3.42	3.29	3.18
27	7.68	5.49	4.60	4.11	3.78	3.56	3.39	3.26	3.15
28	7.64	5.45	4.57	4.07	3.75	3.53	3.36	3.23	3.12
29	7.60	5.42	4.54	4.04	3.73	3.50	3.33	3.20	3.09
30	7.56	5.39	4.51	4.02	3.70	3.47	3.30	3.17	3.07
40	7.31	5.18	4.31	3.83	3.51	3.29	3.12	2.99	2.89
60	7.08	4.98	4.13	3.65	3.34	3.12	2.95	2.82	2.72
120	6.85	4.79	3.95	3.48	3.17	2.96	2.79	2.66	2.56
∞	6.63	4.61	3.78	3.32	3.02	2.80	2.64	2.51	2.41

F distribution:
Upper 1% Points, continued

v_2 \ v_1	10	12	15	20	24	30	40	60	120	∞
1	6056	6106	6157	6209	6235	6261	6287	6313	6339	6366
2	99.40	99.42	99.43	99.45	99.46	99.47	99.47	99.48	99.49	99.50
3	27.23	27.05	26.87	26.69	26.60	26.50	26.41	26.32	26.22	26.13
4	14.55	14.37	14.20	14.02	13.93	13.84	13.75	13.65	13.56	13.46
5	10.05	9.89	9.72	9.55	9.47	9.38	9.29	9.20	9.11	9.02
6	7.87	7.72	7.56	7.40	7.31	7.23	7.14	7.06	6.97	6.88
7	6.62	6.47	6.31	6.16	6.07	5.99	5.91	5.82	5.74	5.65
8	5.81	5.67	5.52	5.36	5.28	5.20	5.12	5.03	4.95	4.86
9	5.26	5.11	4.96	4.81	4.73	4.65	4.57	4.48	4.40	4.31
10	4.85	4.71	4.56	4.41	4.33	4.25	4.17	4.08	4.00	3.91
11	4.54	4.40	4.25	4.10	4.02	3.94	3.86	3.78	3.69	3.60
12	4.30	4.16	4.01	3.86	3.78	3.70	3.62	3.54	3.45	3.36
13	4.10	3.96	3.82	3.66	3.59	3.51	3.43	3.34	3.25	3.17
14	3.94	3.80	3.66	3.51	3.43	3.35	3.27	3.18	3.09	3.00
15	3.80	3.67	3.52	3.37	3.29	3.21	3.13	3.05	2.96	2.87
16	3.69	3.55	3.41	3.26	3.18	3.10	3.02	2.93	2.84	2.75
17	3.59	3.46	3.31	3.16	3.08	3.00	2.92	2.83	2.75	2.65
18	3.51	3.37	3.23	3.08	3.00	2.92	2.84	2.75	2.66	2.57
19	3.43	3.30	3.15	3.00	2.92	2.84	2.76	2.67	2.58	2.49
20	3.37	3.23	3.09	2.94	2.86	2.78	2.69	2.61	2.52	2.42
21	3.31	3.17	3.03	2.88	2.80	2.72	2.64	2.55	2.46	2.36
22	3.26	3.12	2.98	2.83	2.75	2.67	2.58	2.50	2.40	2.31
23	3.21	3.07	2.93	2.78	2.70	2.62	2.54	2.45	2.35	2.26
24	3.17	3.03	2.89	2.74	2.66	2.58	2.49	2.40	2.31	2.21
25	3.13	2.99	2.85	2.70	2.62	2.54	2.45	2.36	2.27	2.17
26	3.09	2.96	2.81	2.66	2.58	2.50	2.42	2.33	2.23	2.13
27	3.06	2.93	2.78	2.63	2.55	2.47	2.38	2.29	2.20	2.10
28	3.03	2.90	2.75	2.60	2.52	2.44	2.35	2.26	2.17	2.06
29	3.00	2.87	2.73	2.57	2.49	2.41	2.33	2.23	2.14	2.03
30	2.98	2.84	2.70	2.55	2.47	2.39	2.30	2.21	2.11	2.01
40	2.80	2.66	2.52	2.37	2.29	2.20	2.11	2.02	1.92	1.80
60	2.63	2.50	2.35	2.20	2.12	2.03	1.94	1.84	1.73	1.60
120	2.47	2.34	2.19	2.03	1.95	1.86	1.76	1.66	1.53	1.38
∞	2.32	2.18	2.04	1.88	1.79	1.70	1.59	1.47	1.32	1.00

Sigma
Conversion Chart

Long-term Yield	Long-term Sigma	Short-term Sigma	Defects per Million
99.99966%	4.5	6.0	3.4
99.9995%	4.4	5.9	5
99.9992%	4.3	5.8	8
99.9990%	4.2	5.7	10
99.9980%	4.1	5.6	20
99.9970%	4.0	5.5	30
99.9960%	3.9	5.4	40
99.9930%	3.8	5.3	70
99.9900%	3.7	5.2	100
99.9850%	3.6	5.1	150
99.9770%	3.5	5.0	230
99.9670%	3.4	4.9	330
99.9520%	3.3	4.8	480
99.9320%	3.2	4.7	680
99.9040%	3.1	4.6	960
99.8650%	3.0	4.5	1,350
99.8140%	2.9	4.4	1,860
99.7450%	2.8	4.3	2,550
99.6540%	2.7	4.2	3,460
99.5340%	2.6	4.1	4,660
99.3790%	2.5	4.0	6,210
99.1810%	2.4	3.9	8,190
98.930%	2.3	3.8	10,700
98.610%	2.2	3.7	13,900
98.220%	2.1	3.6	17,800
97.730%	2.0	3.5	22,700
97.130%	1.9	3.4	28,700
96.410%	1.8	3.3	35,900
95.540%	1.7	3.2	44,600
94.520%	1.6	3.1	54,800
93.320%	1.5	3.0	66,800
91.920%	1.4	2.9	80,800
90.320%	1.3	2.8	96,800
88.50%	1.2	2.7	115,000
86.50%	1.1	2.6	135,000
84.20%	1.0	2.5	158,000
81.60%	0.9	2.4	184,000
78.80%	0.8	2.3	212,000
75.80%	0.7	2.2	242,000
72.60%	0.6	2.1	274,000
69.20%	0.5	2.0	308,000
65.60%	0.4	1.9	344,000
61.80%	0.3	1.8	382,000
58.00%	0.2	1.7	420,000
54.00%	0.1	1.6	460,000
50.00%	0.0	1.5	500,000
46.00%	-0.1	1.4	540,000
42.00%	-0.2	1.3	580,000
38.00%	-0.3	1.2	620,000
34.00%	-0.4	1.1	660,000
31.00%	-0.5	1.0	690,000
27.00%	-0.6	0.9	730,000
24.00%	-0.7	0.8	760,000

Note: The 1.5 sigma shift is included in this chart.

Acronyms

ANOVA - Analysis of Variance - a statistical tool used to analyze variations in a data set

CLT - Central Limit Theorem - it states that the means of random samples drawn from any distribution with mean μ and variance σ^2 will have an approximately normal distribution with a mean equal to μ and a variance equal to σ^2/n

CTC - Critical To Cost - characteristics are product, service, and/or transactional characteristics that significantly influence one or more CTSs in terms of cost

CTD - Critical To Delivery - characteristics are product, service, and/or transactional characteristics that significantly influence one or more CTSs in terms of delivery (or cycle)

CTP - Critical To the Process - characteristics are process parameters that significantly influence a CTQ, CTD, and/or CTC

CTQ - Critical To Quality - characteristics are product, service, and/or transactional characteristics that significantly influence one or more CTSs in terms of quality

CTS - Critical To Satisfaction - characteristics relate specifically to the satisfaction of the customer.

CTX - Critical To X - a flowdown method to help identify the individual x's that can potentially impact the individual y's of a product

DMAIC - Define, Measure, Analyze, Improve, Control - the five phases of the project-focused Six Sigma methodology approach

DPMO - Defects Per Million Opportunities - helps to determine the capability of a process

FMEA - Failure Mode and Effects Analysis - allows an assessment of the risk to customers if a key process input (x) were to fail. The FMEA also helps to determine what actions to take to minimize this risk

KPIV - Key Process Input Variables

KPOV - Key Process Output Variables

LSL - Lower Specification Limit

MSA - Measurement Systems Analysis - used to determine if the measurement system is a significant source of variability and if so, what actions are necessary to repair or replace the measurement system

OCAPS - Out-Of-Control Action Plans

PDCA - Plan Do Check Act - an established improvement methodology referred to as the Plan Do Check Act (PDCA) cycle

QFD - Quality Function Deployment

R&R - Repeatability & Reproducibility - often referred to as part of a test known as a Gauge Repeatability & Reproducibility (Gauge R&R) conducted to determine whether excessive variability exists in the measurement system

RPN - Risk Priority Number - helps prioritize risks based on a risk priority number, where RPN=Probability multiplied by Impact

RTY - Rolled Throughput Yield - used to assess the true yield of a process that includes waste (a hidden factory)

SIPOC - Suppliers, Inputs, Processes, Outputs, Customers - helps to focus the scope of a DMAIC project from the process perspective

SOP - Standard Operating Procedure

SPC - Statistical Process Control

USL - Upper Specification Limit

VOC - Voice of the Customer - used to describe customer needs and expectations

VSM - Value Stream Map - used to identify long-term improvement opportunities to reduce lead time and waste

WBS - Work Breakdown Structure - used to identify the work to be done, it is a hierarchical grouping of project tasks that organizes and defines the total project work

Index

Notes

Notes

Notes

Notes